Lansing
ONE WAY
CHICAGO'S
PIZZA
PICK-UP

John Grant

The Illustrated Lyrics

ABACUS
First published in Great Britain in 2024 by Abacus

1 3 5 7 9 10 8 6 4 2

All songs from Queen Of Denmark, Pale Green Ghosts, Grey Tickles, Black Pressure and Love Is Magic written by John Grant, published by Primary Wave/Blue Mountain/Showpony Music Ltd.

All songs from Boy from Michigan and The Art of the Lie written by John Grant, published by BMG Rights Management (UK) Limited.

A CIP catalogue record for this book is available from the British Library.

ISBN 978-0-349-14730-7
Special Edition ISBN 978-0-349-14731-4

Designed by Sian Rance at D. R. ink
Printed and bound in Italy by L.E.G.O. S.p.A.

Papers used by Abacus are from well-managed forests and other responsible sources.

Abacus
An imprint of
Little, Brown Book Group
Carmelite House
50 Victoria Embankment
London EC4Y 0DZ

An Hachette UK Company
www.hachette.co.uk

www.littlebrown.co.uk

John Grant
The Illustrated Lyrics

Dedicated to
Kristin Ann Dale
for always being there

Contents

Foreword

I love to write songs and I love to take pictures. So this book is a reasonable thing to do, I think.

I have around 70,000 pictures on my phone. So the photos in this book represent just a tiny fraction of the photos I've taken over the years. Some of them I consider to be part of my art and some of them are just ways of remembering where I was and things that caught my eye.

When I first started going out into the world to explore, I didn't have a camera and often wished I had had one to record some memories from all the beautiful places I got to see. I've always been obsessed with moments. I guess that's why I love the photography of Stephen Shore, Bruce Davidson and William Eggleston, just to name a few of my ultimate favorites. They show the types of things that I'm interested in. The little moments, objects, scenarios and details that make up each day and make me enjoy being alive.

Film figures into my work just as much as music and language and I'm a huge fan of the work of Agnès Varda, Wim Wenders, David Lynch, Terrence Malick, John Cassavetes, Rainer Werner Fassbinder, Jim Jarmusch, Charlie Kaufman, Spike Jonze, Mel Brooks, Bruno Dumont, Lukas Moodysson, Stanley Kubrick, Brian De Palma.

Many of these directors are particularly good at shining a light on all the little details that make up a moment so that you feel you are IN the moment. I think that's probably what I think I'm doing with my photos and songs.

I already mentioned my love affair with languages above and I guess that is an obvious one. Language and music are inextricably linked for me. It was usually music which lead me to become interested in learning a particular language. I've spent quite a bit more than half of my life so far loving and studying foreign languages which has led me to try to have a better command of my mother tongue with varying degrees of success. I cannot get enough of words. Like 'squab' for example. Very fun word to say.

Maybe I'm trying to make little films with my music and photos. Maybe I just didn't understand the assignment. It doesn't matter though, I'm just doing what I can to prove I was here. I hope you get some pleasure looking at these words and pictures.

John Grant

Samþyktir
Kaupfjelags Eyfirðinga
Er við daglega
13:30 og

Introduction

You've heard of spontaneous combustion, of course, when someone just explodes and disappears. John Grant can do that just as easily as he can appear out of nowhere, and that's not his only talent.

The word polymath is almost as overused as the word awesome, but John is both these things. I think these photos are up there with Lartigue and Diane Arbus. Oh, and Weegee. Weegee was a famous photographer/photojournalist in the '40s and '50s. He was notorious for always being first on the scene of a major crime, hence his nickname which was derived from the word Ouija. I reckon the mob tipped him off to their antics. In much the same way, John Grant always seems to be in the right place at the right time, either writing, playing the piano, singing, or wielding a camera.

I have always adhered to the maxim that poetry is poetry and lyrics are lyrics and that lyrics should not be read but listened to. There's an exception to every rule and John is it. His lyrics read like stream of consciousness, Joycean with an Idaho twist. Oh how I wish I could love like he does.

John and I have forged a great friendship, which consists of walks, eating baked cheesecake, and taking photographs. John always takes pix. I am hopeless at pix. Everyone ends up headless. I'm the poor woman's Duchess of Argyll.

It is always a good idea these days not to be florid whilst writing about someone's work. Well, fuck that shit. If it's pretentious to ooh, ahh and swoon, then knit me a hat with a big P. on it. John's work is momentous and demands big reactions, n'est ce pas? Okay, maybe a French phrase is pretentious.

And now, for your delectation, I am going to interview some poems.

J.G. And I feel just like Winona Ryder, in that movie about Vampires, and she couldn't get that accent right, and neither could that other guy.

L.T. Oh that drives me mad.

J.G. But it's easier for me, to believe that you are lying to me, when you say you love me

And when you say you need me.

L.T. Much easier.

J.G. I still don't know, what I am looking at, 'cause I've never seen anything like this before

I have a friend, who's an astronomer, and he says he cannot help me, 'cause he doesn't have a clue.

L.T. A summation of life.

J.G. Jesus, he hates Fruit Loops son, we told you that when you were young, and pretty much anything you want him to, like sitcoms, pedophiles and kangaroos, morons who cut in line, three-bean salad and parking fines and when we win the war on society, I hope your blind eyes will be opened and you'll see.

L.T. Indoctrination is hard to shake off but you did it.

J.G. I'm usually only waiting
For you TO stop talking so that I can,
Concerning two-way streets
I have to say that I am not a fan.

L.T. Finally, someone said it.

J.G. Remember how we used to fuck all night long?
Neither do I because I always passed out
I needed lots of booze, to handle the pain.

L.T. Hasn't everyone experienced this?

J.G. On a warm June summer night
A car pulls up and Cindy's sittin' on the passenger side
Her hair was dirty and she had the prettiest eyes
And she was in possession of one of those million dollar smiles.

L.T. I was looking particularly good that night.

J.G. So many people chasin' Sacagaweas
Me I'd rather have a bunch of
Onomatopoeias baby.
Thwap Splat Gurgle Gurgle

L.T. Kapow!

J.G. I was

Boning UP on my Icelandic declensions

When the landlord rang me up and said you

Don't get no extentions that's a bitch

Come on baby, that's a bitch

Come on suga, that's a bitch

Come on baby, that's a bitch.

L.T. Dear Landlord, please don't put a price on my soul. (Thanks Bob)

J.G. You're not THINKING, you have trouble with that

You think you're super special but you're just a thick twat

You probably went to Chernobyl for your honeymoon

You probably acted surprised when they showed you the room.

L.T. An irradiating image.

Linda Thompson

Queen of Denmark

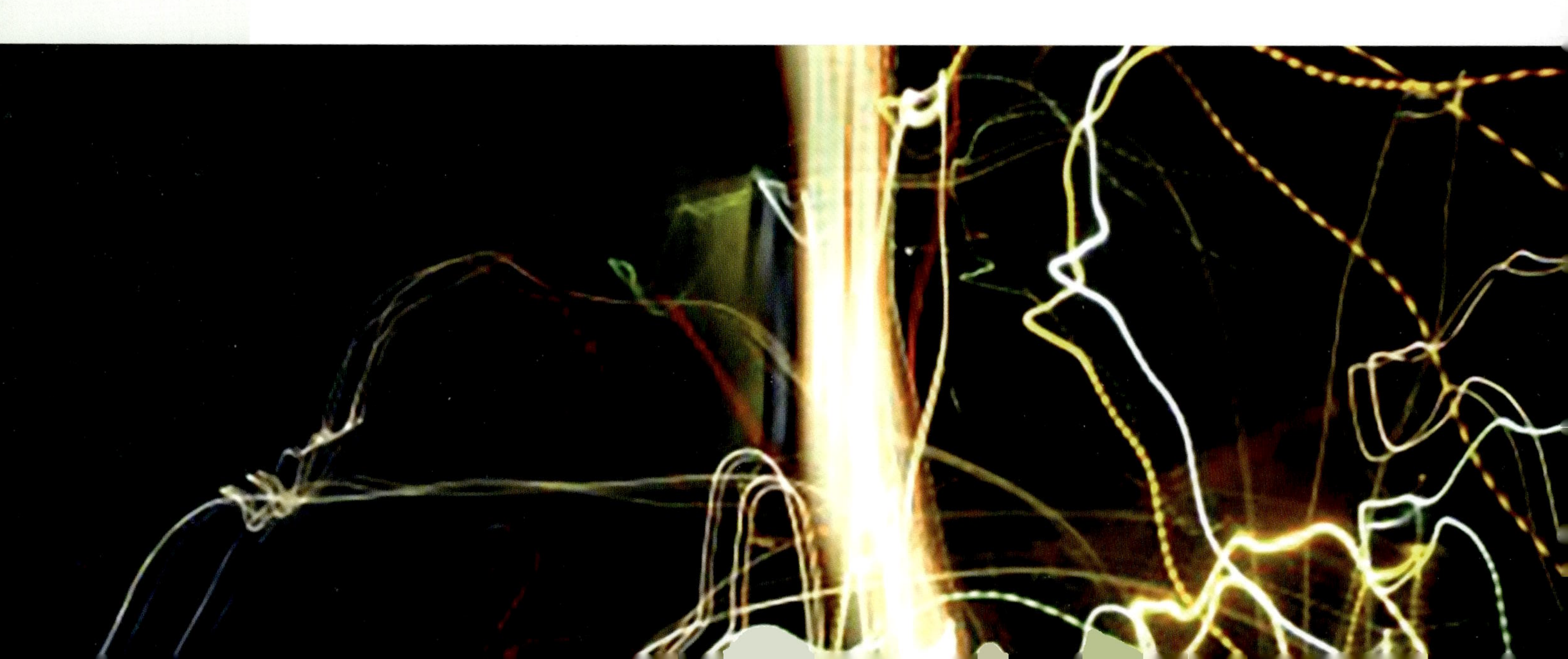

TC and Honeybear

For TC and his Honeybear, the world will not stop moving, for rendezvous
and longing stares, and hearts that won't stop yearning
Before that Honeybear had given up, he felt so sad and lonely,
Then one night he looked up and he saw, he saw his one and only

When TC came onto the scene, he entered in on golden wings
And with him he brought butterflies, of crimson red and emerald green
'Cause before TC Honeybear was waiting, was waiting for him patiently
TC took his fear away, became his one and only

The world came crashing down on them, with all of its ferocity, and
Honeybear was terrified, he said do not take him take me
Before that Honeybear had given up, he felt so sad and lonely
And then one night he looked up and he saw, he saw his one and only
And he said please don't take him, 'cause I love him, he's my joy and my life

For my Love, I won't hesitate, I will give him all that his heart can take
And I'll trust him fearlessly, I want him to be free

Marz

Bittersweet Strawberry Marshmallow Butterscotch, Polar Bear Cashew,
Dixieland, Phosphate, Chocolate
Lime Tutti Frutti Special, Raspberry, Leave it to Me, Three Grace, Scotch
Lassie, Cherry Smash, Lemon Freeze

I wanna go to Marz, where Green Rivers flow, and your sweet sixteen is
waitin for you after the show, I wanna go to Marz, you'll meet the Gold
Dust Twins tonight, you'll get your heart's desire, I will meet you under
the lights

Golden Champagne, Juicy Grapefruit, Lucky Sundae, High School Football,
Hot Fudge Buffalo, Tulip Sundae, Almond Caramel Frappe, Pineapple,
Root Beer, Black and White, Big Apple, Henry Ford, Sweetheart, Maple
Tear

Where Dreams Go to Die

Your beauty is unstoppable, your confidence unspeakable, I know you know, I know you know, that I know that you know, I'm willing to do anything, to get attention from you Dear, even though I don't have anything that I could bargain with

This IS like a well-oiled machine, could I please see that smile again, it's all that makes me feel that I am living in this world, I see you closing all the doors, I see the walls as they go up, I know it's what you have to do, I'd probably do the same thing too, my Dear

Baby, You are where Dreams go to Die and I regret the day, your lovely carcass caught my eye, Baby, You are where Dreams go to Die, and I've got to get away, I don't want to but I have to try, Oh Baby

You have to play your part my Dear, I've written it all down for you, it doesn't matter if the words you say to me aren't true, just do it then I'll let you go, just say the words and say them slowly, I promise I'll tell no one, yes I cross my heart and hope to die

Sigourney Weaver

When I woke up today, the air was very strange, I couldn't feel my skin and
there was evil in my bones, I tried to speak but found that I didn't have a
voice, it was a prison like the one you would find in the Twilight Zone

And I feel just like Sigourney Weaver, when she had to kill those aliens, and
one guy tried to get them back to the earth, and she couldn't believe her
ears

So I was taken or I went towards what was West, to where the ground was
dead and struck out at the giant sky, the sky was black and filled with tiny
silver holes and it was there with a frightened voice that I began to cry
out loud

And I feel just like Winona Ryder, in that movie about Vampires, and she
couldn't get that accent right, and neither could that other guy

And I feel just like I am on Jupiter, the one that looks like Rainbow Sherbet,
but it doesn't lend itself to life, and I haven't finished yet

All of a sudden, I felt as if I belonged.

J
451090000-1
W-2

Chicken Bones

When I got out of my bed this morning, I noticed that it didn't have a right side
And my head felt like it's filled to the top, with Pop Rocks and Cyanide
There's an earthquake coming and you think you know, where it started, but it started very long ago, I need a Mongoose Baby and some Calgon, to take me up out of here.

Some Days Just Chicken Bones, you better fuck off now, you better leave me alone, 'cause I'm about to explode just like a Wonder Bread bomb and I don't care what I know, because I can't be wrong

Yes I know why you need it, 'cause your car broke down, and you wanna take the next bus outta this town, but if anybody's gettin' on the bus, dawg, it's gonna be me
I know I don't need what you got for me, but maybe I do, theoretically, you better watch out Sugah, 'cause I'm about to get my Old Spice on

Some Days it's just Chicken Bones, you better fuck off now, you better leave me alone, 'cause I'm about to explode just like a Wonder bread bomb and I don't care what I know, because I can't be wrong
Some days it's just Chicken Bones, I'm all jacked up on DC at my place alone and I don't care what you think about my attitude, because I can't be bothered with the likes of you

Silver Platter Club

I wish that I could get up in the early morning time and things would fall
out of the sky into my lap, I wish I had the brains of a Tyrannosaurus Rex,
so that I wouldn't have to deal with all this crap
I wish that I'd been born with skin that turns a golden brown, while at the
beach relaxing in the summertime
I wish that I was good at Football, Baseball and Lacrosse, Darts and
Basketball and Poker, Golf and Chess

I'm sorry that they didn't hand it to me on a Silver Platter like they did to
you
I'm sorry that I wasn't able to become, the man you think I should aspire to

I wish I had the genes of Eduardo Verastegui, that I was effortlessly
masculine as well, I wish that confidence was all you could see in my
eyes, like those interviews in locker rooms with talented sports guys
I wish I had no self awareness, like the guys I know, who float right through
their lives without a thought, and that I didn't give a shit, what anybody
thought of me, that I was so relaxed you'd think that I was bored

I'm so sorry...

It's Easier

I don't know who I thought I was, I guess I tried to love you, because I thought I could afford, to take the risk and take a chance
I do not know who I thought I was fooling, I must have felt invincible in your arms, like I could take the whole world on

But it's easier for me, to believe that you are lying to me, when you say you love me
And when you say you need me
Yes it's easier for me, to walk away and get on with my life, if I believe that you're deceiving me, if I believe that you'd be leaving me one day, be leaving me one day, be leaving me some day

I wish that I could make you see, but clearly that is not to be, 'cause you will not be swayed by me, you've made it clear, you must be free
I would've sacrificed for you, I would've been so loyal and so true, but gifts this precious can't be offered up by fools
And it's easier…

What's done is done I cannot change the way I feel and what's more I am certain that I don't regret a single thing, but sometimes I really miss your sweet sweet love, and wish that I'd wake up and this would all be just a dream

Yes, it's easier…

Outer Space

I still don't know, what I am looking at, 'cause I've never seen anything like this before
I have a friend, who's an astronomer, and he says he cannot help me, 'cause he doesn't have a clue

I think that you must be from outer space
Maybe from somewhere beyond the stars
I think you must be extraterrestrial
'Cause you can open up the heavens for me
With just one smile

What is that sound, coming out of your mouth
'Cause I've never heard anything like that before
It sounds like a language from another galaxy
I want to thank you 'cause you opened the door

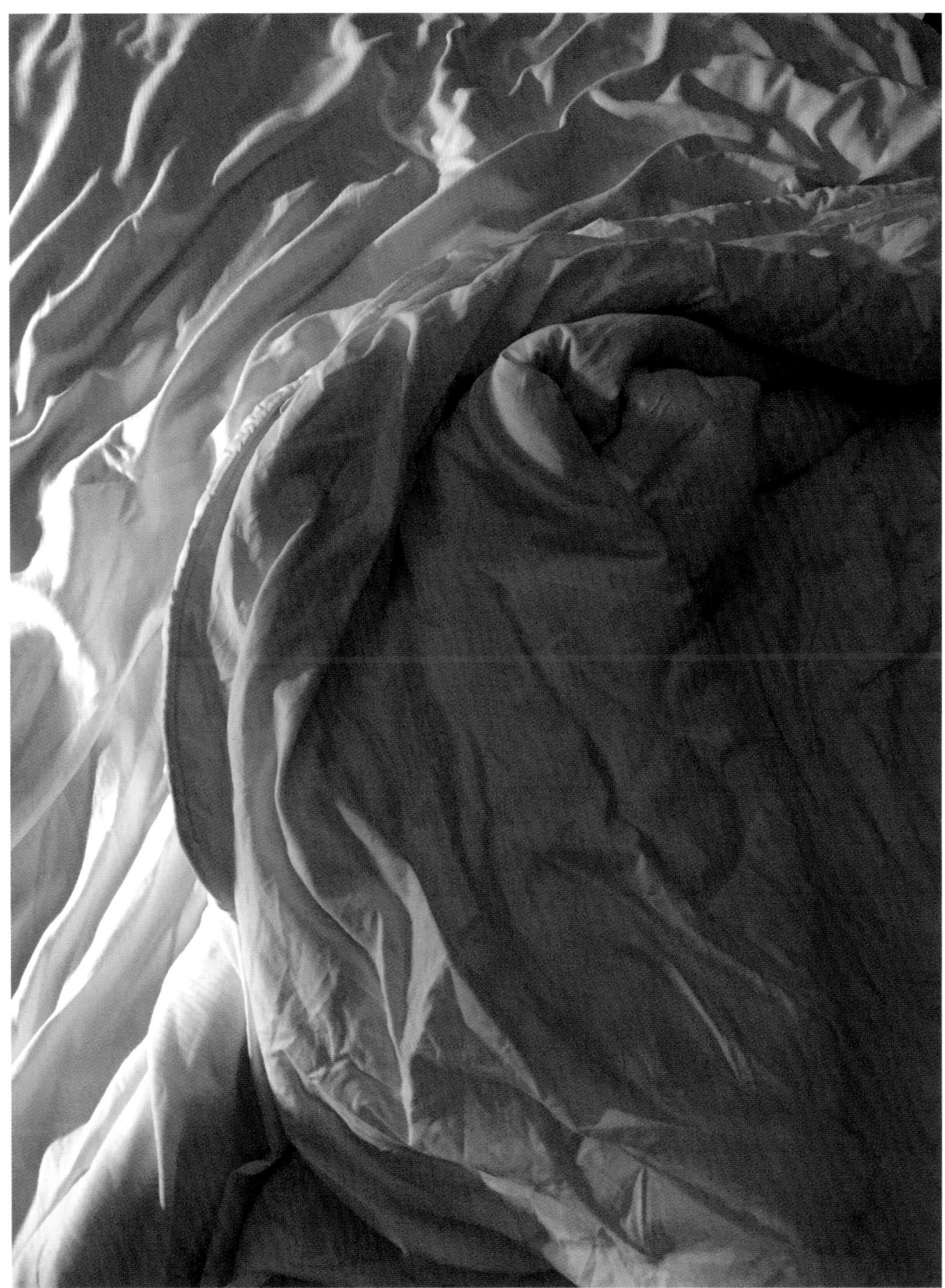

A barn owl manifested in my sheets in Madrid.

Jesus Hates Faggots

I've felt uncomfortable since the day that I was born, since the day I saw the black abyss in your eyes, there's no way you could make all of this shit up on your own, it could only come from the mastermind of lies

I can't believe that I've considered taking my own life, 'cause I believed the lies about me were the truth
It will be magic to watch your transformation when you realize that you've been had, it's enough to make a guy like me feel sad (almost), 'cause you tell me that

Jesus, he hates Fruit Loops son, we told you that when you were young, and pretty much anything you want him to, like sitcoms, pedophiles and kangaroos, morons who cut in line, three-bean salad and parking fines and when we win the war on society, I hope your blind eyes will be opened and you'll see

The arrogance it takes to walk around in the world the way you do, it turns my brain to jelly every time, the rage and fear I'm feeling have begun to make me sick and I think that I might be about to commit a crime

And you tell me that

Jesus, he hates Homos son, we told you that when you were young and pretty much anything you want him to, like Coco Puffs, red cars and Jews, postal clerks who waste your time, weight-loss shakes and the local news and when we win the war on society, I hope your blind eyes will be opened and you'll see

'Cause Jesus, he hates Faggots son, we told you that when you were young, and pretty much anyone you want him to, like N******, Spics, Red Skins and Kykes, Men who cannot tame their wives, weaklings, cowards, and Bull Dykes and when we win the war on society, I hope your blind eyes will be opened and you'll see

MARTHA'S
DANDEE CREME
AND
Grill

HOWDY
DOODY
DRIVE-IN
BEER
WINE
GROCERY

Caramel

My Love is the rarest Jewel and he crowns me with his love,
My Love, he is rich, like Caramel and he moves me from above
He sees me with Tiger Eye eyes and that's where I make my home
His heart is a shield, which protects me from the vilest foe,
His smile is an elixir, which heals the wounds of my darkest years
When my Love is quiet, I consider him and he drives away my fears

My Love, he reveals himself, with tenderness and grace
My Love has constructed with his arms, for me, the safest place
His Laughter destroys my doubts and lifts me up so high
His Voice it is soothing, like a warm breeze on a summer night
When he envelops me I give myself to him and my soul takes flight

Leopard and Lamb

I read your letter and finally I could cry, but I don't really understand exactly why
I guess I cried, 'cause I knew it was the end, no more hating now, just learning to begin

Learning how to crawl across, a floor that's covered with glass (broken, jagged), learning how to look away and never to look back

I cannot fathom, how it dragged on for so long, and I think we both know which one of us was wrong, and now I'm asked to act as if I didn't feel, anything for you my friend and it's a bitter pill to swallow

You're right, this world is cold and all that I can do, is banish any thought of you, because you are so cruel

I watch the Simpsons, to remember how you laugh, I miss your dark blue eyes and staring at your back, my Leopard, my Lamb

You're right, this world is cold and all that I can do, is banish any thought of you, because you are so cruel
Like learning how to crawl across the floor that's covered with glass, like learning how to look away and never to look back

Queen of Denmark

I wanted to change the world, but I could not even change my underwear
And when the shit got really, really out of hand, I had it all the way to my hairline
Which keeps receding like my self confidence, as if I ever had any of that stuff anyway
I hope I didn't destroy your celebration, or your bat mitzvah, birthday party or your Christmas
You put me in this cage and threw away the key, it was this us and them shit that did me in
You tell me that my life is based upon a lie; I casually mention that I pissed in your coffee
I hope you know that all I want from you is sex, to be with someone who looks smashing in Athletic wear
And if your haircut isn't right, you'll be dismissed, you'll get your walking papers and you can leave now

I don't know what to want from this world; I really don't know what to want from this world
And I don't know what it is you want to want from me, you really have no right to want anything from me at all
Why don't you take it out on somebody else, why don't you bore the shit out of somebody else
Why don't you tell somebody else that they're selfish, a weakling, coward, a pathetic fraud

Who's going to be the one to save me from myself, you better bring your
stun gun and perhaps a crowbar, you better pack a lunch and get up
really early, and you should probably get down on your knees and pray
It's really fun to look embarrassed all the time, like you could never cut the
mustard with the big boys, I really don't know who the fuck you think
you are, could I please see your license and your registration

So Jesus isn't coming here to pick you up, you'll still be sitting right here ten
years from now
You're just a sucker, but we'll see who gets the last laugh, who knows maybe
you'll get to be the next Queen of Denmark

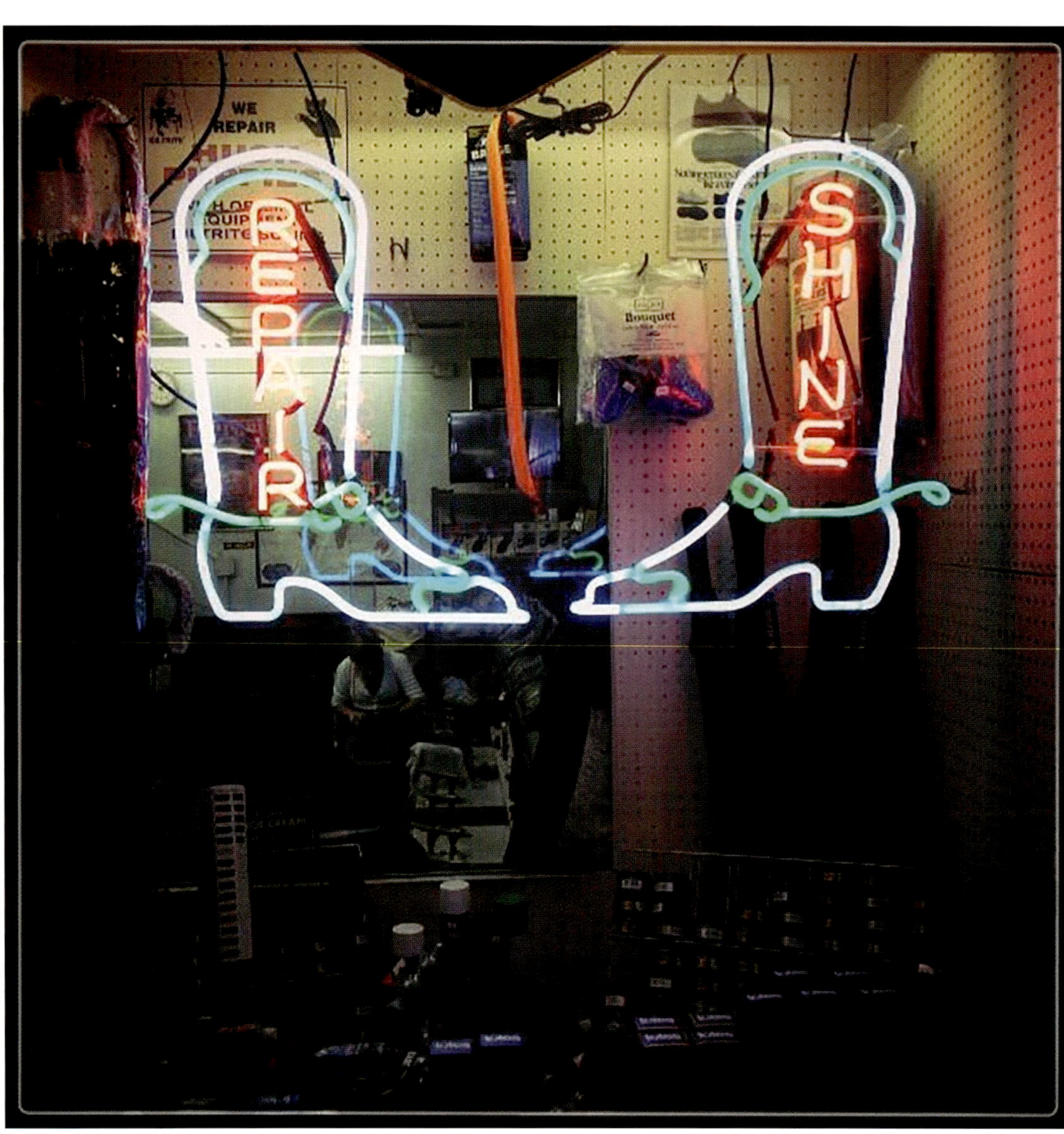
WE
REPAIR
REPAIR
SHINE
Bouquet

REPAIRS
Deposit is Necessary
NOT RESPONSIBLE FOR GOODS LEFT OVER 30 DAYS
CAVALIER SHOE CR

That's the Good News

Yeah, um... Hello Tony

You cannot trust me I will stab you in the back
I'll sell your grandma on the street to buy some crack
If crack is not available I'll buy gelato
You have to take things as they come that is my motto
I'm laying groundwork for your ultimate demise
But you can't see that when you look into my eyes
I have been fucked over a thousand times or two
And now I feel that I must take it out on you
And that's the good news
that's the good news, baby
When you talk to me I am vomiting inside
I think that vomit is what killed my inner child
When I look at you I am filled with violent rage
I feel like telling you that you should act your age
All I can talk about is your ineptitude
And how that little ass of yours looks just like food
Your taste in clothing is of no concern to me
It's just a reflection of your stupidity
And that's the good news
that's the good news, baby
Das sind die guten Nachrichten
das sind die guten Nachrichten, Baby

Supernatural Defibrillator

Boy you knock me on my ass so hard
How could I know that you was holding that ace card
When I saw you my jaw hit the floor
Now I don't want them other boys no more
You sent a laser beam of love to my soul
You made me shake so hard I lose control
My sweet director won't you give me the part
'Cause you're the one who jump started my heart
'Cause you're my supernatural defibrillator
You are my heavenly re-animator
You are my super sexy stimulator
You are my loneliness exterminator
Come on baby 'fore I come unglued
Don't make me wait boy that would be so rude
You got me where I always wanted to be
Right in front of you and down on my knees
I feel like someone punched me right in my head
I need to lay down baby take me to bed
You leave me gobsmacked, dumbfounded, twitterpated
Bound and struck, stunned and shot, fuddled, discombobulated
'Cause you're my supernatural defibrillator
You are my heavenly re-animator
You are my super sexy stimulator
You are my loneliness exterminator
You're my supernatural defibrillator

You are my heavenly re-animator
You are my super sexy stimulator
You are my loneliness exterminator
'Cause you're my supernatural defibrillator
You are my heavenly re-animator
You are my super sexy stimulator
You are my loneliness exterminator
You're my supernatural defibrillator
You are my heavenly re-animator
You are my super sexy stimulator
You are my loneliness exterminator

Fireflies

On a summer night, 1975
Maybe earlier, now I don't remember
She catches fireflies at the ice cream social
And oh
We watch them take flight
He is coming now with the rake on fire
He destroys the nest of the wasps up high
We are standing there with the fire in our eyes
And oh
We don't know what we're seeing
At the cemetery back beyond our house
There's a grave with pictures, one of him, one of her
I can smell the flowers, they died long ago
And oh
How I long for you...

DOEPFER
External CV/Audio Inputs
A-110 VCO
STANDARD VCO
Range
Tune
CV2
PW
PW CV2
DUAL VCA
A-126 VCFS
VC Frequency Shifter
Audio In
Level
Overload
Shift
Audio Out
A-138 MIXER
In
exp
Input 1
In1
In2
Out
A-127 VCRF
DOEPFER
DOEPFER
DOEPFER

Pale Green Ghosts

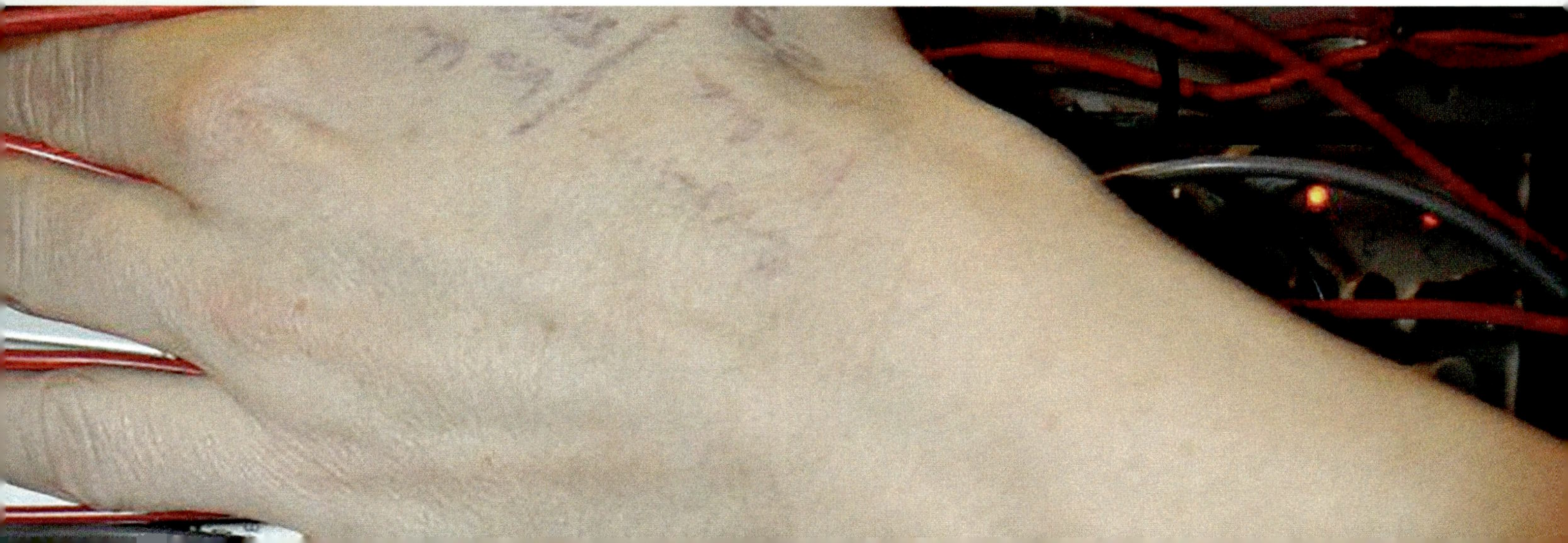

Pale Green Ghosts

Back then I often found myself
Driving on the road at night
And the radio was broadcasting the ocean
Warm late spring wind whips through my hair
I am right here but I want to be there
And no one in this world is going to stop me

Pale green ghosts at the end of May
Soldiers of this black highway
Helping me to know my place
Pale green ghosts must take great care
Release themselves into the air
Reminding me that I must be aware

I-25 and 36 to Boulder
I was getting warm but now I'm getting colder
And I stomp my feet, demanding like a child
I hope you get everything you wanted boy
I hope you conquer the world and turn it into your toy
But don't come crying when you're forced to learn the truth

Black Belt

You are at the top of your game aren't you?
Would you not say that you agree, baby?
You got your grift all fine-tuned and sparkling
Yeah, you got your bored look all worked out
You are all enlightened, nothing makes you frightened
You ain't got no time to waste on entry-level middle class
You are super-silly-ESS (supercilious), pretty and ridiculous
You got really good taste you know how to cut and paste

What you got is a black belt in B.S.
But you can't hawk your pretty wares
Up in here any more
Hit your head on the playground at recess
Etch-a-Sketch YOUR way outta this one, reject

You know how to get what YOU want DON'T you
Would you not say that YOU agree baby
You really think that you can school me in semantics
I can't recommend that baby, I see through your antics
You think you're mysterious, you cannot be serious
You got lots of time to think up new ways to deceive yourself
You are callipygian, but look at the state you're in
You got really nice clothes, bet you didn't pay for those

SMILE
YOU'RE ON CAMERA

GMF

You could probably say I'm difficult,
I probably talk too much
I overanalyze and overthink things,
Yes, it's a nasty crutch
I'm usually only waiting
For you TO stop talking so that I can,
Concerning two-way streets
I have to say that I am not a fan

But I am the greatest motherfucker that you're ever going to meet,
From the top of my head down to the tips of the toes on my feet
So go ahead and love me while it's still a crime,
And don't forget you could be laughing 65% more of the time,
You could be laughing 65% more of the time,

Half of the time I think I'm in some movie,
I play the underdog of course
I wonder who they'll get to play me
Maybe they could dig up Richard Burton's corpse.
I am not who you think I am,
I am quite angry which I barely can conceal.
You think I hate myself but it's you hate
Because you have the nerve to make me feel

I should have practiced my scales
I should not be attracted to males

But you said that I should learn to love myself
Well, make up your mind Dr. Frankenstein

But I am the greatest motherfucker that you're ever going to meet,
From the top of my head down to the tips of the toes on my feet
So go ahead and love me while it's still a crime,
And don't forget you could be laughing 65% more of the time,
You could be laughing 63% more of the time,
You could be laughing 25% more of the time

CACHET
to
GM
by

Vietnam

To say that I'm a man undone
Is understatement at its worst
I was completely incapacitated
By your southern charm
It hit me like an ancient gypsy curse
But this instrument you use with such precision
It's like a concrete wall, a thousand meters tall
And I've tried to climb its icy walls a million times
But I simply cannot find inside of me
The requisite resolve

Your silence is a weapon
It's like a nuclear bomb
It's like the Agent Orange
They used to use in Vietnam
And it's accompanied by an apathy
Which is deafening to the ears
You know it IS complete and perfect
And you wield it without fear

It isn't complicated, you just don't care
You attack me by not saying anything
You say that you don't bring your anger to me
But it poisons ever fiber of your being
Now you've started something that you cannot finish
And left me standing in the wreckage on my own
And the only thing that brings me any comfort
Is the knowledge that no matter who you're with
You'll always be alone

It doesn't matter to him

If I think about it,
I am successful as it were
I get to sing for lovely people
All over this lovely world

And I'm no where near as awkward
As I was when I was younger
I guess I'm one of those guys
Who gets betting looking as they age

And even though I have felt beaten down
By constant doubt, depression and confusion
Brought about by people's actions, death and tax forms
I keep getting up and I am loved by all my friends and family
Though there have been lots of raised eyebrows,
And concerned glances lately

(However)

It doesn't matter to him,
I could be anything
But I could never win his heart again
It doesn't matter to him,
He took away my triple A pass
I am invisible to him

And now I feel the soft pink flesh
Of my heart hardening
To the countless possibilities
Contained within each day
Vulnerability feels like
A cold, wet, concrete room lit
With fluorescent lighting,
Which as you know
Makes everything look bad
I still keep tryin' to figure out
How I became irrelevant
How I got myself evicted
From his heart from one day to the next
AND the worst part is,
That even if I got an answer right now
It would not change anything
Because we have become two strangers

Why Don't You Love Me Anymore?

My friends all say that you're no good
That you're not fit, to shine my shoes
They say that you are not, the caliber of man
That I deserve to have
Well, I don't know that much about guns
But I feel like I've been shot by one
I am ashamed, 'cause I don't know myself right now
And I am 43

The knowledge that I can't be what you need
Is cutting off my air supply
And yet this information has not reached my heart
And that's why I still try
They say that I should go outside more
And drink lots of water all the time
But that does not seem to be working
'Cause you still have not come back to me

Why
Don't you
Love me
Anymore, tell me why
Don't you
Love me anymore

I feel like telling everyone
To fuck off all the time
'Cause they don't know
I keep expecting Woody Allen
To jump out, from those dark shadows
I watched Jane Eyre last night
And thought about which role
Would work the best for me
My mind is tired, and all I'm doing now
Is worrying my friends and family

Why
Don't you
Love me
Anymore, tell me why
Don't you
Love me anymore
Just in case
You didn't
Hear me ask before
Tell me why don't you
Love me anymore...

ふか川
ろの味
☎ 932-1221

You Don't Have To

Remember walking hand in hand, side by side?
We walked the dogs and took long strolls through the park,
Except we never had dogs, and never went to the park

Remember how we used to fuck all night long?
Neither do I because I always passed out
I needed lots of the booze, to handle the pain

You don't have to pretend to care
You don't have to say things that you don't mean
You don't have to pretend to care
You don't have to say things that you don't mean
It just embarrasses me, and makes you look like a fool

Remember when the tenderness stopped?
And the kindness turned to pity and disgust?
And the smiles were stopped, before they could start?
And understanding was now just a tool, we used it every
Chance we got to be cruel and we cringed because,
We couldn't make ourselves stop

There are days when I think about you
And on those days I really feel like a fool, because
You don't deserve, to have somebody think about you
I feel so stupid, 'cause I let myself down
I acted like a mother fucking clown at a circus
On the outskirts of town

You don't have to pretend to care
You don't have to say things that you don't mean
You don't have to pretend to care
You don't have to say things that you don't mean
It just embarrasses me, because you think you're so FUCKING COOL!

Davis
Purity
Bakery

Sensitive New Age Guy (ode to Schwa)

Take Picasso, Otto Dix and add some Salvador Dali
Accompanied by Wagner plus some Public Enemy
She isn't any of these things, and she would never want to be
She is a special kind of thing made from a secret recipe

He had a deeper understanding of the state that we are in
She didn't run away and hide, she stayed right to the bitter end
He demanded our attention and we tried to do our best
She was taking us to school, but most of us would fail the test

She's just a sensitive new age guy
You came to the wrong place, if you came to see her cry
If you have the guts then please look deep into her painted eyes
You could be a better human she just wants to see you try

He always played the good cop to her fabulosity
Where she had been they had to replace light bulbs constantly
'Cause she could always only be the brightest in the room
She had a special way of preaching glamour mixed with doom

With just a simple quip she'd wipe that smirk right off your face
And replace it with a smile while demonstrating latex grace
And with time I saw him less and less I don't know where he went
But it was I who ran away to some far foreign-speaking place

She's just a sensitive new age guy
You came to the wrong place, if you came to see her cry
If you have the guts then please look deep into her painted eyes
You could be a better human she just wants to see you try

Ernest Borgnine

How much is enough?
That's a really tough question,
You ought to give it some thought
Sooner or later
Got off of the hooch and the crack, and skipped the smack-down
But then you had to find yourself a lower low

Doc ain't lookin' at me says I got the disease
Now what did you expect, you spent your life on your knees
It was never too late tell me what are you afraid of
Do the numbers in your head or get out your calculator

I wonder what Ernie Borgnine would do
I got to meet him once and he was really really cool
And when I think about everything that he's been through
I wish he'd call me on the phone and take my ass to school

Sorry that you think you've had it tough in the first world
You ought to get out a map sooner than later
Knowledge has turned into a trap, you have to slow down
Get out of your head and spend less time alone

But you never learn you get your labyrinth on
You lay awake at night and think that you are getting old
You don't need to panic now you got time to do that later
You're the Jack who's chasing Danny lost out in the snow

I Hate This Town

Horrifying as it was for me
To see your face today
(I guess) I knew that IT would happen at some point
(And) I dreaded it because I knew
That you would be so kind
You're good at that you've got it right down to a science

So you observe the strict rules laid out in the books of etiquette
And TELL me you hope I enjoy my stay
And I feel numb and can't believe
That I was stupid enough to leave my bed today
If I'm so smart then why is this happening?

You know I hate this fucking town,
You cannot even LEAVE your fucking house
Without running into someone who no longer cares about you.
Somebody whom you desperately want to see
But you know it's only GOING to cause more grief
'Cause there's nothing left to say
And he can't hear you anyway.

It's so confusing 'cause I really want to hate you
But my intellect reminds me that that doesn't make no sense.
And I wanted to be your friend but I couldn't pull it off in the end
And I'm disappointed with myself because I thought I could.

But then again you always made it clear,
That you do not care either way, which begs the question
How can I still claim to love you
You told me time and time again that you don't lose you always win
And that to MAKE an effort WOULD just be beneath you.

Now I'm packin' my bags again, and you are not inside of them

CARWASH

Sorp

Glacier

You just want to live your life
The best way you know how
But they keep on telling you
That you are not allowed
They say you are sick
That you should hang your head in shame
They are pointing fingers and want you to take the blame

There are days when
People are so nasty and convincing
They say things beyond belief
That sting and leave you wincing
And to boot they say their words
Come straight down from above
And they really seem to think that what they're
Doing counts as love

But this pain, it is a glacier moving through you
And carving out deep valleys
And creating spectacular landscapes
And nourishing the ground
With precious minerals and other stuff
So do not become paralyzed with fear

Don't you pay them fuckers
As they say no never mind
They don't give two shits about you
It's the blind leading the blind
What they want is commonly referred to
As theocracy
What that boils down to is referred to as hypocrisy
Don't listen to anyone
Get answers on your own
Even if it means that sometimes
You feel quite alone
No one on this planet
Can tell you what to believe
People like to talk a lot
And they like to deceive

CITY OF DALLAS

Grey Tickles
Black Pressure

Grey Tickles, Black Pressure

I did not think I was the one being addressed
In hemorrhoid commercials on the TV set
I often stand and stare at nothing in the grocery store
Because I do not know what to buy to eat anymore

And parapraxis is the order of the day
I'd never heard that word until tonight I have to say
And I'm supposed to believe that there's some guy who'll take the pain away
But there are children who have cancer, and so all bets are off
'Cause I can't compete with that, so all bets are off,
'Cause I can't compete with that...

I've got Grey Tickles and Black Pressure
And I'd rather lose my arm inside of a corn thresher
Just like Uncle Paul, Just like Uncle Paul
ahhhhhhhhhhhhhhhhhhhhhhhhhhhhhhhh

And they won't be happy til they tear down everything
Which looks remotely cool, or is older than two weeks
You must be kidding me, except I do know better than to ask

I can't believe I missed New York during the 70s
I could have gotten a head start in the world OF disease
I'm sure that I would have contracted every single solitary thing
But there are children who have cancer, and so all bets are off
'Cause I can't compete with that, so all bets are off
'Cause I can't compete with that

They say let go, let go, let go, you must learn to LET GO!!!!
If I hear that fucking phrase again, this baby's gonna blow
Into a million itsy bitsy tiny pieces don't you know
Just like my favorite scene in Scanners
Apparently there was an outcry of some sort today
Which no one heard, incidentally and by the way
I have not HAD the strength to leave my place in days or weeks
And I'll never understand what's happening in the Middle East
But there are children who have cancer, so all bets are off,
'Cause I can't compete with that
So all bets are off, 'cause I can't compete with that...

TAXIS

Snug Slacks

Is it difficult for you, to be so beautiful?
Or do you find the advantages tend to outweigh
The disadvantages?
Am I being rude? I'm sorry, I've never really
Had the appropriate attitude

Do you think that life is easier
When one looks as good as you do
Or do people always say that you're
A narcissist
Do they ingratiate themselves to you
And act all obsequious
Come on now baby, you can tell me
It's just between the two of us

Snug slacks, Baby, snug slacks
Now you're givin' me a different kind of panic attack
I said, sick joke, Baby, crack smoke
Now take me out in your pickup for a midnight poke
I said, Stonehenge, Baby, drug binge
Now you got me all damp, down in my netherlands
Snug slacks, Baby, snug slacks, now let's get you out
Of those and see what kind of punch your manhood
Packs

You know it takes an ass like yours
To make it possible for me, to have developed
Such a very high tolerance for
Inappropriate behavior, I mean
I can take it or leave it, I don't need it
And I hope I haven't spoken out of turn
But if you'd be so kind, I could use some help
With my thesis on CARPET BURN

By the way, I got tickets for us to see Joan Baez tonight
Oh, I guess I misunderstood, I've never hear of
Joan as Policewomen, but I do love me some
Angie Dickinson, AND let's be clear: Joan Baez makes
G.G. Allen look like Charlene Tilton

Guess How I Know

You laughed all the way through Ordinary People Baby
That's how I knew
Something ain't right, there's no other way to say it Baby
There's somethin' wrong witchoo

You made a crazy scene at the Dairy Queen
Only Blood Sausage will do
I didn't like in Germany
And I ain't'a'gonna start likin' IT for you

Guess how I know you are a Zombie baby
'Cause you ripped my heart right out of my chest
You don't exhibit any feelings Baby
You're as cold as ice it's obvious you're dead

You got real rambunctious at the restaurant
You wouldn't stop throwin your food
People gonna start spreadin nasty little rumors Baby
If you don't find a way to fix your mood

Your bedside manner makes me wanna watch Cujo baby
For the 20th time
But it kinda gets me hot, kinda hits the spot
I guess it's, it's gotta be an unforgivable crime

Auf Wiedersehen Baby
Bon Débarras
I'll catch you on the flipside, Honey
Do Svidaniya

You and Him

You're so hot, I bet you hear that a lot, uh huh
You're so cute I almost wish I were you
You're so slick it's like you're not even tryin'
You're so cute but can you tell that I'm lyin'?

You're so sweet
But you remind me of somebody else
It's on the tip of my tongue, no, it's not
Orson Welles
You're so ambitious, you just know you're
Gonna win
You're so cute, I hope they taught you how to swim

You and Hitler oughta get together
You oughta learn to knit and wear matching sweaters
You oughta, learn the finer points of decoupage
You oughta spend your weekends cleaning out the garage

You and Hitler oughta tie the knot
You could do it at Taco Bell to spice up the plot
Get on the phone and call your buddy Pol Pot
You could, play some Twister
And watch Heavy Metal Parking Lot

You're so cute, I really love how you hate
You seem like someone they should chemically castrate
I bet you're planning to have seventeen kids
Then two nano-seconds later you'll regret that you did
Because:
You're not THINKING, you have trouble with that
You think you're super special but you're just a thick twat
You probably went to Chernobyl for your honeymoon
You probably acted surprised when they showed you the room

GAS

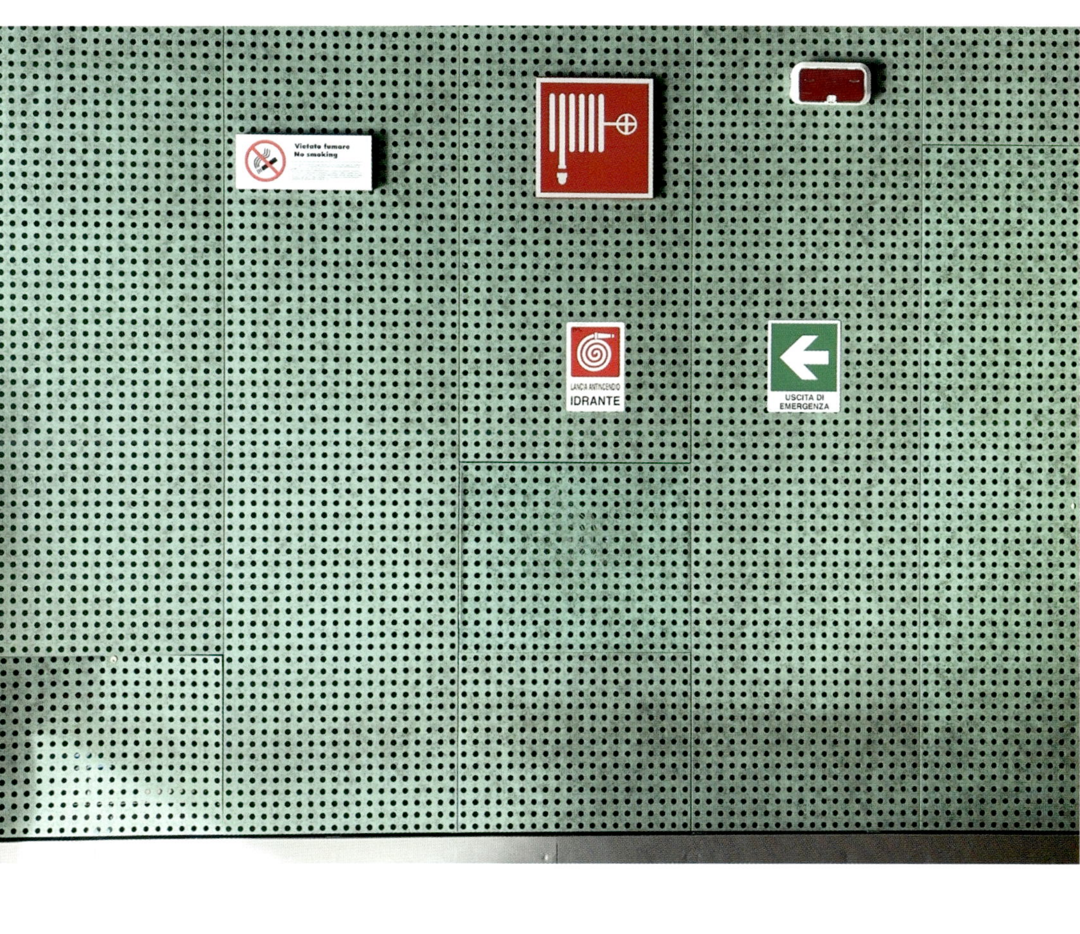
Vietato fumare
No smoking
LANCIA ANTINCENDIO
IDRANTE
USCITA DI
EMERGENZA

Down Here

You do this, you'll get that
I want what I was promised
I'm a bit impatient
And what is it exactly, that you think
That you deserve
No more, no less
Is that ridiculous

'Cause what we got down here is
Oceans of longing, and guessing games
And no guarantees
And you worked so hard to be in control
And now you're laughing at yourself
'Cause you can't let go

And all we doing, is learning how to die
Do you really think, nobody sees the fear
Behind your smile
And why do you care, what anybody thinks at all
It's all going to the same place in the end

Voodoo Doll

You can't get out of your bed
Because you're so depressed
No one understands this and they
Think that you're a mess
I know this is not the case and I
Believe in you
I won't stop until I have convinced
You of the truth

I made a voodoo doll of you
Then I gave it some chicken soup
Did you feel any warmth down deep inside
Did you feel how your blues went away
And died
I made a voodoo doll of you
I even put it in a corduroy jumpsuit
'Cause I thought that's what you would do
If you had the opportunity to choose

Even on your worst day I hate no one less
Than you
Break into my house and read my diary
If you need some proof
You are going to make it and you'll do much
More than that

Just don't stop just keep on moving
There's no turning back

I made a voodoo doll of you
Then I gave it some chicken soup
Did you feel any warmth down deep inside
Did you feel how your blues went away
And died
I made a voodoo doll of you
I even put it in a corduroy jumpsuit
'Cause I thought that's what you would do
If you had the opportunity to choose

I made a voodoo doll of you
And I administered hot chocolate too
One time I spilled it all over the place
I really hope you don't got no
Burns on your face
I made a voodoo doll of you
I didn't know what else to do
I know you don't get out that much
So I took it on a trip to Kalamazoo

Global Warming

You people and your cute little terms
You like to throw them around to make everybody squirm
Upper class, middle class, lower class, sassafras,
Everybody these days thinks that they're a badass

And how am I supposed to live in a world
With no Madeline Kahn, my favorite girl is gone
And Bonnie Doon's is now an AutoZone
31 is trashed, and now I just want to be left alone

Global Warming
Is ruining my fair complexion
Augmenting all my imperfections
And Brazil does not need more encouragement
Global Warming
Encourages slack-jawed troglodytes
To leave their homes with guns and knives
In search of quality refreshments and some homicide

I'm so sick of hearing people talk about the sun
They sound like a bunch of Aztec Indians
And all they do is hang out clogging up the streets
Congratulating each other on their pedicured feet

Sure I like to see the fellas skateboard in their vans
Strip down to their shorts, so they can work on their tans
I know I shouldn't care 'cause I'm a taken man.
But I guess you can look
Nobody said that you can't...

Magma Arrives

We see our hero in his chambers now
Luxuriating on a water bed
He should enjoy it if he can somehow
'Cause soon he'll wish that he were dead

Did you hear the one about the monkey's paw
Some people dig that sort of thing
Well this will be much worse I promise you
He'll never see another spring

Magma arrives
With fire in his eyes
And says it's time to fill our hero's veins
With shame that runs so deep it makes
Impossible his sleep
Affecting countless destinies and lives

Your face will melt right off your skeleton
You see his bite is much worse than his bark
You cannot take it back, you've made your bed
This won't be no damn walk in no damn park.

You won't be able to hide anything
There will be no place to put the blame
It's almost tempting to feel sorry for you now
But can you guess what is my name.

LAFAYETTE ST
DAIRY TREAT
STOP

PEPE'S
CORNER
LIQUOR
$11.99
UNITED WE
SUMMER
12 Pack
Cans
Corona
Extra
$20.99
KEYSTONE LIGHT & ICE 30 PACKS
Modelo
Modelo
15.99
12 PK
CANS

Black Blizzard

Grasslands, sweet Grasslands
This will be our home
We will work the soil and wait
Because we know our time
will come

Black Blizzard
Souls will wither
Crushing hearts and bones
Black Blizzard
Eternal winter
Will you forsake your own

Blue Sky Sunday morning
We welcome back the sun
Maybe we'll have peace now
The conquerors have won

Black Blizzard
Souls will wither
Crushing Hearts and Bones
Black Blizzard
Eternal winter
Will you forsake your own

Black Blizzard, Chicken
Gizzard
Daddy had to go
He crawled five blocks
In the Devil's black snow…

GAS

ITALGAS
GAS

GAS

Disappointing

Roller coasters and Earl Grey malts
Ocelot babies, but not bath salts

A harvest moon in the arms of a tree
Which has been growing there for centuries

Bassoons, trombones and French horn sections
Bass clarinets and string art collections

Owls and good socks when they do not match
Gilda, Kristen, Cheri, Tina, Amy AND Rachel Dratch
(Jan, Maya, Molly, Jane, Nora, Ana, Laraine, Julia)

All these things, they're just disappointing
All these things, they're just disappointing
Compared to you
There is nothing more beautiful than your smile
As it conquers your face
And there is nothing more comforting than to know
Know you exist in this time, in this place

The Genitive case, in German, it's true
Is something that I am quite partial to
Rachmaninov, Skriabin, Prokofiev
Dostoevsky, Bulgakov, Vyssotsky and Lev

Frances Bacon and the Dolomites
Ballet Dancers with or without tights
Central Park on an autumn day
Will always be stunning and never cliché...

No More Tangles

Stockholm is a place that I adore
But the syndrome by that name
is one that I abhor.
Patty Hearst cannot compete with me.
I bet she thinks she can.
I'll prove her wrong a.t. for free.

Words don't mean anything to you.
Emotions turn right into lies, like black turns into blue
Because the fear has made you blind
You don't know anything
You thought that I was being kind...

No more tangles, no more tears (my dear)
No more reindeer games with narcissistic queers
Or any other such type of human being
No more angles, no more, dumbing it down
Gee your hair smells terrific but I cannot stand to have you around
Not now, or any other time

This is a metaphor for fear
Answers to questions, you've been asking me for years
And what of adrenaline fatigue?
I've got a lot of that.
Just tell me, how much do you need.

You spend your days tied up in knots
You know how to tie them in your flesh and in your thoughts
Even without reading Moby Dick
Tell me how does one, learn that at your age
So that it sticks

BURGER &
HOT DOG
CHIPS
Coca-Cola

VELKO

Geraldine

The paranoia, the uncertainty
The stupid, knowing way they're grinning when they look at me
They say it's me, how do they know
My mind and body have betrayed me and it shows.

The brain reboots each time
The sun begins to shine
And if I didn't know better
Then I'd swear to you that it's not mine
I can't control my face
I can't avoid that furrowed brow
I would've thought they'd send someone
Right over to show me how

Geraldine
Please tell me that you didn't have to put up with this shit
Geraldine
Please tell me that you didn't have to do it, like the others
We're not like them, we're not that strong
At least that's what they have been telling us all along
Geraldine, please tell me that it wasn't like that for you

You are a grown up now
The program is complete
And everybody knows this
Because of the things you say when you speak
You know the drill
It's time to kill
And if you don't they'll find somebody else who will

This is a hostile world
Don't act like you weren't told
Nobody's gonna buy that noise
If you talk like that when you get old
Don't lose your cool
Don't come unglued, be a man
Don't walk into the light, it's a trap dear Carol Anne

Love is Magic

Metamorphosis

Acid Trips and globs of gravy
You'll transform there is no maybe
Glaciers calfing, have you met the smiler
Married to the Nothingness, don't tell Granny Kyler

14-year-old boy rapes 80-year-old man
Tickets to the Met, sweetcorn from a can
Baby's in the Whitest House playing with his toys Earthquakes, forest fires, Hot Brazilian Boys!!!
67 yogurt flavors, which one do you want?
Can't decide on toothpaste, Immanuel Kant
Do you really think, they don't know what they're doing? Everything was O.K., someone needed screwing
Yeast infection, synthesizer, demisemiquavers
who created ISIS?
Emotional blackmail (she knows what I mean)
Broccoli with cheese sauce, how long you been clean?

As I enjoyed distraction, she just slipped away
It didn't seem to matter, how much she had prayed
They took her in, an ambulance, and that is where she died
And still, unto this very day, I don't think I have cried
About my selfishness, my self-absorption
Questions left unanswered, spiritual extortion
And in my dreams, her face is vague, a mere suggestion
And when I wake, I can't remember, why I'm feelin' sad

A new shooting, fresh for breakfast
This one's in Florida, not in Texas
Manchurian candidate, cute subconscious trigger
Have you seen the remake, I have to watch my figure
Lemon Bismark donut, that will hurt now won'it
Tiki bar, rat soufflé, Buik regal, Marvin Gaye
Synthia Cylvia, would not take the garbage out
Now just look what you've done, your delicious secret's out
Whirl-A-Whip, Blood Lust, who do you think you can trust?
Empire Crumble, Calculated Stumble
Are you ready for your Black awakening?
You're not gonna wear THAT, are you Doctor Fakenthing
Do you know what they did that fateful night on Jekyll Island Rockefeller
Salad, Sandy Dunkan smiling
It's almost as if you always knew what's coming
Harken to the wind, you can hear the faintest drumming...

Vocabulaire progressif du Français
débutant
PHONÉTIQUE PROGRESSIVE DU FRANÇAIS
Grammaire Progressive du Français
débutant
GRAMMAIRE PROGRESSIVE DU FRANÇAIS
CLE

Love is Magic

Have you got depression?
Passive aggression?
Did they stop loving you
And you're the only one who doesn't know? You forgot your medication
And Sade is playing on the radio

They say you were always enough
It's too ridiculous to call their bluff
And you're staring at a dresser drawer
which is devoid of clean underwear
You're tryin' to work out on your calculator
If you can swing that trip to anywhere but here

Love is Magic
Whether you Like it or Not
It isn't so tragic
It's just a lie that you bought
When the door opens up for you
Don't resist, just walk on through
There is nothing left to lose

Do you think you can take the pain
Is it destroying the inside of your brain
And you've come so very far to hear
That you're nowhere near half-way there

There's no milk in the refrigerator
And you'll be hearing all about it when you
Get home tonight

And this thing called intimacy
Is it what you always thought it would be
Do you feel like you've experienced
What the word is supposed to mean?
Do you feel like you are in control?
Did you find out that there's really
No such thing?

Tempest

In the halls and in the
  churches
They were preening on their
  lofty perches
Indulging their conspiracies
And they were looking
Right at me

Come play Tempest with me
Or maybe Millipede
We can while away the hours
Away from the hordes
I've almost reached
The yellow boards

I hear the doors of institutions
Opening and slamming shut
They were desperate for
  solutions
They were drowning In their
  elocutions

Come play Tempest with me
Or maybe Centipede
We can hang out in the mall
It's where I feel at home
I don't want to be alone

Come play Tempest with me
Or maybe Centipede
We can hang out in the mall
Away from the hordes
I've almost reached
Those nasty green boards

Preppy Boy

He wore cuffed khakis, crisp and clean
Brown topsiders and
He doesn't use sun screen
Navy blue polo shirt
Why you chasin' that girl In the whale skirt

I see you, out there
Playing lacrosse, I
I know, you wanna be the boss, and
As far as I'm concerned you can, but
You know, she'll never understand

Come on now preppy boy
If you've got an opening, then I am unemployed
I'm so sick and tired of waiting in line
Call me up if you're down, and you've got the time

He wore a candy-striped button down
He's got laser white teeth
They sparkle like a crown
He's got highlights in his hair
From the sun of course

I gave him my number
So that after the divorce
He could, call me up
If he wants to chat

You know, I've waited so long and
Now I'm up to bat,
he's no Treat Williams
But neither am I
It might be wishful thinking
But you've got to try, now...

Smug Cunt

It's in the way you stare
Your obsession with your chest hair
I can smell it in your choice of cologne

I can't believe it's real
Neither can you, 'cause you can't feel
Your smile cuts right through to the bone

You don't care who you hurt
Just the right amount of starch in your shirt
You don't want things you cannot own

The only thing that you're aware of
Is anything you can't be above
You don't believe you reap what you have sown

But now you're just a smug cunt
Who doesn't even do his own stunts
They just let you in 'cause you won't shut up
You're still acting like a little boy
Masturbating with expensive toys
They just let you play 'cause you won't shut up

All the girls think you're a stud
Even though your hands are covered in blood
And they're turned on by your cover ups

The highest compliment is being feared
I bet that you don't even think that's weird
You don't care who your deeds corrupt

But now you're just a smug cunt
Who doesn't even do his own stunts
They just let you in 'cause you won't shut up
The protein's flying off the shelves
Them panties ain't gonna wet themselves
They just let you play 'cause you won't shut up

It would be funny if it weren't so sad
It's so absurd it's gonna drive you mad
And you still believe that there's an us and them

Do you know anything that you weren't told
Have a think 'cause you are getting old
You don't even try to cover up the stench

He's Got His Mother's Hips

I think Colonel Mustard
Did it in the billiard room
Yeah yeah

They say his salsa workshops
Are a harbinger of doom
Yeah yeah

He's takin' itsy bitsy
Super pointy stipsies
Straight to the middle of the Dancefloor

He does the Hokey Pokey
Now the room is getting smokey
He won't read you your rights
Before they turn out the lights

He's got his mother's hips
He does the dippity dip
He's got delicious quips

He's got his mother's hips
He thinks he's going downtown
And now he's smacking his lips

He. Does. Not. Speak Your.
Language.
Watch your back
His tongue is super dangerous

He's got his thigh-highs
And his roller-skates ON
You are rolling the dice
He wants you on thin ICE

He's serving cheese fondue
ON the polar bear rug
But the room is bugged

You got MESMERIZED by the
lava lamp
But now the carpet's damp
He's tryin' to sell you some
stamps

He's got his mother's hips
He's on an ego trip
He's got sartorial tips

He's got his mother's hips
He thinks he's going
downtown
And now he's smackin' his lips

He's got his mother's hips
He does the dippity dip
He's got delicious quips
Now baby

He's got his mother's hips
He thinks he's goin'
downtown
And now he's smackin' his lips

Diet Gum

I manipulate, that is what I do
I manipulate, that's what I'm doing to you
That smirk on your face was designed by me
I fucking curated it like, magically
I manipulate, that is what I do
I manipulate, that's what I'm doing to you

You don't like what I've become?
What'd you expect to happen?
You come around here with your lips a'flappin'
All hopped up on Diet Gum
And everything you say is 'sposed to make me come

Like, I should feel grateful you are in my life
But I'd rather dig out my own spleen with a butter knife
Hey!!! I've got some Gainesburgers you can have if you want 'em
You might as well, you've clearly hit rock bottom

You probably hang out at Times Square with Maytag Blue in your pocket
And around your neck is your grandmother's locket
With a picture inside of what you might have been

SOUND FAMILIAR?!?!?
Do you even know where that cheese is made?
It's from Iowa, you DULLARD! EVER HEARD OF IT?!?!

I know this guy from Ames, Ames, Iowa, Patrick
Who would SO not be into you in THE most extreme way

By the way, your bedside manner
Is reminiscent of a chuckle of hyenas except...
Yes it IS a chuckle of hyenas Dr. Turd Face
It's a collective noun
Do you even know what a collective noun IS, Stupid-Zilla?!?!

Hmmmmmmm
Let's see, I think your group would be called a "misery"
Or, NO, a "Patheticness" of Fuck-wits
OH, oh right, pardon me your royal doofessness
A patheticness of BARISTAS

I manipulate, that is what I do
I manipulate, that's what I'm doing to you
That smirk on your face was designed by me
I fucking curated it like, magically
I manipulate, that is what I do
I manipulate, that's what I'm doing to you

You know, being with you
Was like a cross between Cannibal Apocalypse and Lassie 9,
Except nowhere NEAR as good as both of those movies were
It's still a personal conundrum of mine
How ANYONE could have such few of self-awareness

I manipulate, that is what I do
I manipulate, that's why you just took a poo
In those slacks you're wearing

Is that a leisure suit?
Did you make that yourself, that's a rhetorical question

I manipulate, that is what I do
I manipulate, it's rather easy with you
You're sort of begging for IT with your stupid face
You're like Daffy Duck about to be erased

Did you really think you could seduce me in a leisure suit?!
Well, I, uh, yeah, ok, fair enough, but that was like three weeks ago
I'd like to see you try that now

I'm not staring at your crotch, you Maynard, I am NOT
Well, it's hard not to, I mean,
You practically dislocated your own hips thrusting it at me
You're like that neon sign that keeps Kramer up all night
Yeah, I guess you did keep me up all night a few times.

Really? 463? How could you know that?
We only went out for a year.
What? Um, I dunno, I was just gonna order out, uh, I was gonna...
Well, sure, I guess so

Hey, um, I'm sorry I sorta
Snapped at you a few minutes ago
Uh, it's nothing personal, I hope you know that

Is He Strange?

Licorice and nuts
There are no ifs and
There aren't any buts
He was just there
He was just standing there
He was on an island
In the North Atlantic Ocean
Just minding his own
He was just doing his thing
And in that moment
Everything changed

Is he strange
Or is it you, who never
Saw the light?
Decades of everything wrong
Give way to everything right
But that don't mean that it will stick
He's not some flower you can pick

Purples, reds and blues
You act like you have
Never read the news
Now you must choose
What are you going to do?

It's just good to know that
You can love while you are
Letting go, look at the snow
Look at it swirl and blow
And you never thought
That tree would grow

Brown Norwegian cheese
Don't worry who you do
And do not please
At the very least
You've got other dead horses
to beat
You can't win or lose
You simply are, and that's how
He is too, and you're never
Through, nobody said that
It would be smooth
Now close your eyes
And concentrate on this
Groove

Is he strange
Or is it you, who never
Saw the light?

Decades of everything wrong
Give way to everything right
Baby you're not strange
You are the only one
Who's ever been right
I'm just sorry that I let you
down
And that's what keeps me up
at night
(not just the Common Snipe)
And I only hope that you can
see
That you transformed
This heart inside of me

The Common Snipe

Jill and I were talking Just the other day about the Bower birdies
And the little houses they make
They collect sticks and objects in lovely colors
In order to attract a special and suitable lover

David thinks the Hummingbirds are fascinating
I wonder if they invented the art of speed-dating
They flap their wings 50 to 200 times per second
I guess that's how they get those crazy pecs

But it was the flight of the Common Snipe
Which kept me up in my bed at night
And I thought about what it was to him
A reflection of his beauty which made my head swim

Have you ever seen a picture of a Cassowary?
It has a six-inch claw which I find rather scary
If you're not careful it may very well eviscerate you
And if you ask me that's a dinosaur

And what is UP with the Shoe-billed stork?
It looks like it's about to stab you with a fork
And yet apparently it's highly prized
Perhaps because its' beak is very large in size

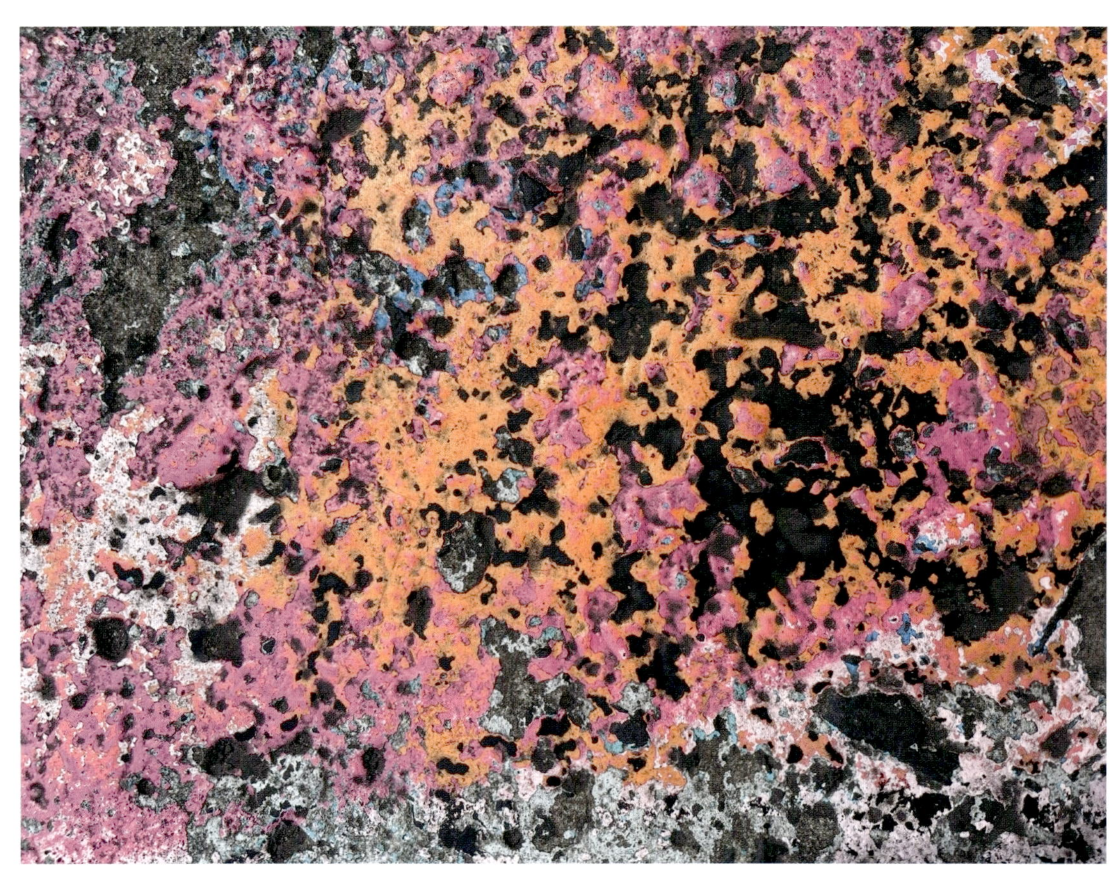

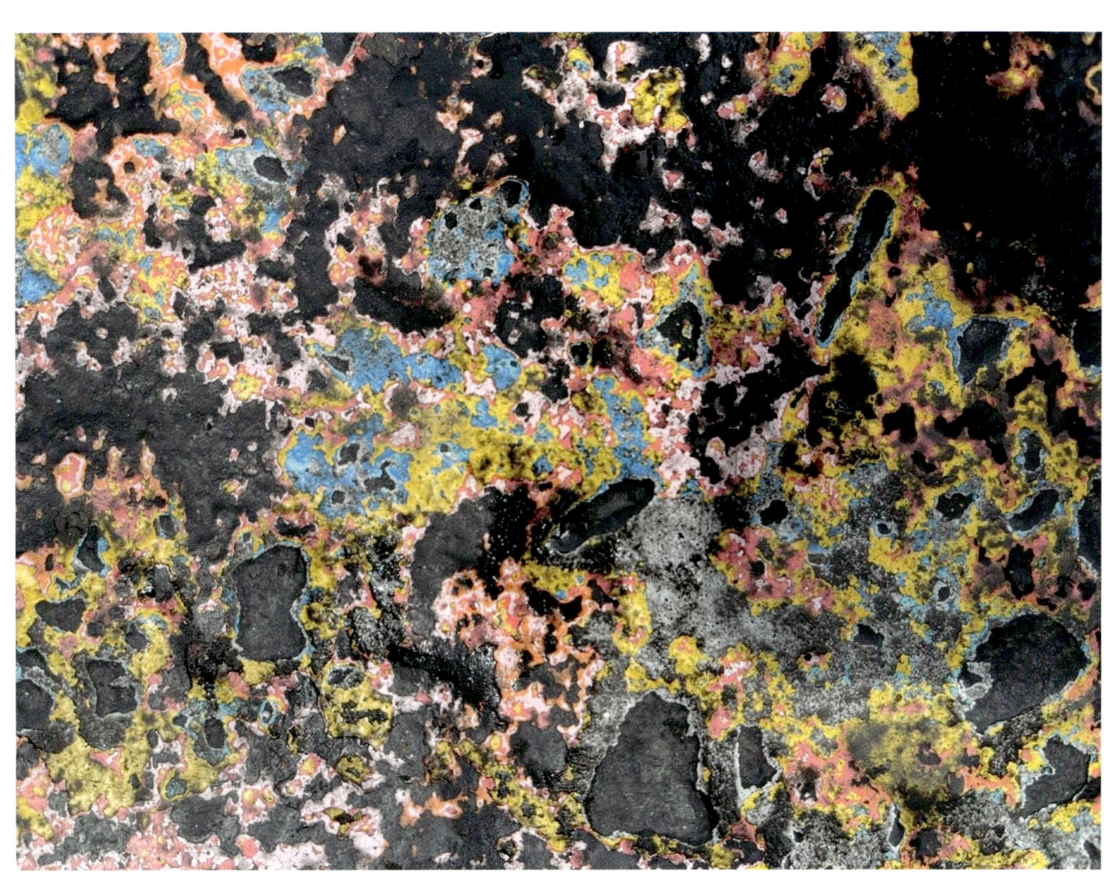

Touch and Go

What have they been telling you
About the way things are?
Could you have foreseen back then
That you would come this far?
It was touch and go there for a while
Don't you agree?

Did you play with Barbie dolls
When no one else was around?
Pardon me if I sound ignorant
But the change is so profound
What was going through your head
As they struck you down to the ground?

What they think is patriotic
Barely passes for robotic
And not one of them could last
Three minutes in your shoes
The darkness almost swallowed you up
That must have been quite a case of the blues

I know that I'm supposed to be
Incensed by what they say you've done
But I only feel compassion 'cause
They're liars, every one
You've been keeping secrets all your life
But now you are done

Chelsea is a butterfly, she metamorphisized
You can't catch her with your net
'Cause she is free inside
You can't stop the progress of the truth
Try as you might

Boy From Michigan

Boy From Michigan

You know my mother sewed clothes for Bertha Wrunklewich
That lady who I always thought was rich and I considered her
With awe and wonder when she came around

And in the summertime we went to Catherine Park
A place where you could have yourself a summer lark
Swinging and spinning on the merry-go-round,
Til the sun went down.

And I was haunted by the stories about Connie's car
And how she barely got out when it caught on fire
And a trucker came along and he saved her life and
She was alright

Now it sits across the way from Hall's Apple Farm
A place that I have carried with me for so long
You can find it if you drive along Red Bud Trail
through the Maple trees. (in the Autumn time)

Beware, when you go out there
They'll eat you alive if you don't take care
They have different rules they're using
The American Dream can cause scarring
And some nasty bruising
Beware, when you go out there

They'll eat you alive if you don't take care
They're using different rules
The American Dream, if not for weak,
Soft-hearted fools

And all the neighbor boys
They got them permanent waves
And we walk through the cemetery
Looking at all the graves
To Thompson's market, for candy and pop
We did it almost every day

We used to look to see if we could find a patch of green
As the Winter came to a close and Spring
Was blossoming, the ground was comin' alive
And it smelled so clean…

And Scotty said softly, with some sadness in his voice
You're just a simple boy from Michigan
And they'll be doing everything they can to win
So please, please don't ever let your guard down
And maybe someday you can come back here again

County Fair

On a warm June summer night
A car pulls up and Cindy's sittin' on the passenger side
Her hair was dirty and she had the prettiest eyes
And she was in possession of one of those million dollar smiles

And I can hear the leaves lush and green up in the trees
And they are whisperin' to a gentle breeze
Cindy says "Come on we're goin' to the county fair,
You can ride with us, or we can meet you there."

We'll ride the Zipper and the Tilt-A-Whirl
We'll watch the cotton candy twist and swirl
We'll ride the Matterhorn and the double Ferris-Wheel
We love to listen to the screams and the squeals
And it's hard to believe, that the things we are seeing
Are real

Cindy takes my hand as I start to cry
They say I'm too small and they won't let me ride
I look up at the Zipper as it twisted and writhed
I saw all the lights reflected in their eyes.
I will never forget, the things I saw that night.
I felt so much love and everything was alright.
And she said, "Come on we're goin' to the county fair
You can ride with us, or we can meet you there."

The Rusty Bull

On the way out of town on
Old Walton road
There's a twenty foot rusty bull
With a ring right through its nose
If you ask all the folks in town
Some of them remember, but
Most of them don't
He guards the entrance to the junkyard
Where my daddy goes.

His eyes fill my heart with dread
And he visits me, while I lie in my bed
He says: "Your daddy can't undo what's done"
And 40 years later I'm still trying to run

I wake her up in the middle of the night
I plead with her and I present my plight
But I see a weary melancholy in her face
And I understand that the Bull is right.

And the stairs still creak at the Five and Dime
And it smells like something set apart from time
And I see you smiling at the Tastee Freeze
And the sun's goin' down behind the Maple trees

Now the bull stands under ice and snow
And the Winter offers no reprieve
The moon is tangled up in the branches of the trees
And he won't let me leave

Spring is the promise that never came
The bull tightens his grip and I curse his name
Now every morning is a harsh reminder
That everything is the same...

The Cruise Room

I see you in the pink art deco glow of the Cruise Room
I see you not knowing all the things we didn't know
At the Cruise Room, way back then

Patsy Cline on the juke box and I don't wanna hear
Nothing else
We leave the world outside and the fear begins to melt

They can't touch me, as long as you are by my side
This is the place we come when we know we have to
Say goodbye

I remember later on that night, sitting by myself
Back at home
We listened to that song over the phone
And I knew I'd never be alone
And the wind outside
It howled and moaned

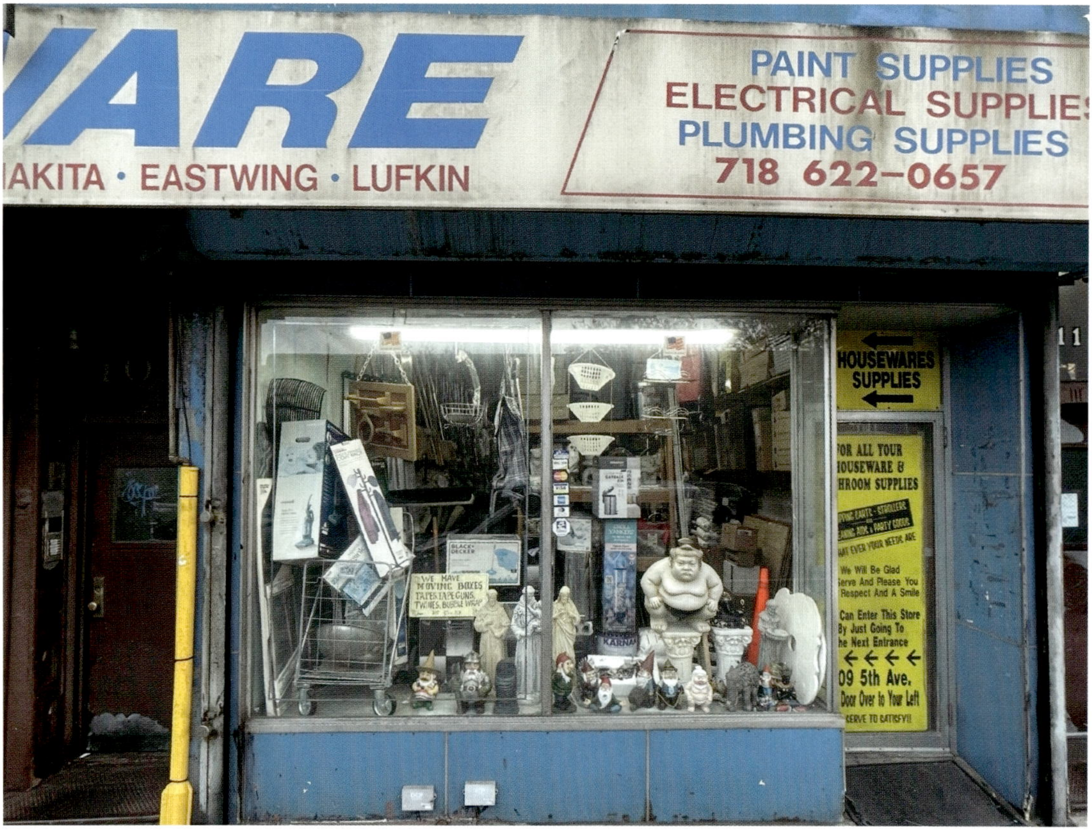

EASTWING · LUFKIN
PAINT SUPPLIES
PLUMBING SUPPLIES
718 622-0657
HOUSEWARES
SUPPLIES
FOR ALL YOUR
HOUSEWARE &
We Will Be Glad
Respect And A Smile
Can Enter This Store
By Just Going To
Next Entrance
WE HAVE
MOVING BOXES

VISA

Mike & Julie

On a lonely, back-country road, just outside of
Shawnee, In Oklahoma
The bass line of our song on your cassette
Sounds like the storm clouds we see up ahead
On the horizon

When we get to the place we are going
I look at the floor as I search for some words
I don't want to hear what I think you might say
You know what you want and I'm much too afraid
And I, only feel shame and that makes me feel rage
At myself

Mike, can you hear me, are you out there Mike,
Mike, are you listening, I'm sorry

Julie's a force which must be reckoned with
She's kind and she's strong and she shoots from the hip
Her laugh is what you did not know you were missin'
And if you are smart and try real hard to listen
You'll learn from her what friendship is
And what it isn't

Now Julie is coming and she'll be here soon
She'll be my escape from the truth in this room
And I know that I can't run away all my life
But I will be damned if I'll let someone else
Decide who I am, or who I'll become

Julie, are you out there, I've been thinking about you Julie
Are you listening? I miss you.

On a lonely, back-country rode, just outside of Shawnee
In Oklahoma

CLEAN UP
CLOSED

Best In Me

Titania's Fritillary
Camouflaged Looper
Scarce Chocolate Tip

Coxcomb Prominent
Northern Apple Sphinx
Lettuce Shark
Poplar Kitten

You bring out the best in me
So I can function as I want to be
Because, You bring out the best in me
So I'll be cancelling my killing spree

Small Ranunculus
Honey Suckle Bee
Hawk Moth
Yellow Spot Jewel

Chryxis, Arctic
Pygmy, Hermit
Tawny Prominent
American Dagger

Rhetorical Figure

Some people like alliteration
But I have always been an
Assonance man

Ah-Ee-Ah-Oh-Ah
Ah-Ee-Ah-Oh-Ah
Ah-Ee-Ah-Oh-Ah-Ah-Ah
Ah-Ee-Ah-Oh-Ah
Ah-Ee-Ah-Oh-Ah-Ah

Some people like to go on vacation
I decline and conjugate, therefore
I am

Essen-Aß-Gegessen
Flechten-Flocht-Geflochten
Gießen-Goss-Gegossen
Klingen-Klang-Geklungen
Helfen-Half-Geholfen

If you want to get with me
You better have a
Rhetorical Figure, a
Rhetorical Figure, if
You want to get up ON
This you better have a
Rhetorical Figure, A
Rhetorical Figure

Rhetorical Figure (Rhetorical Figure)
Rhetorical Figure (Rhetorical Figure)

Epizeuxis, Epizeuxis, Epizeuxis, Epizeuxis
We use it a lot, but the spelling kinda
Spooks Us

Your constant employment of analogy
Is a turn-on that is certainly not lost on me

You're an expert when it comes to using
Paraprosdokians, unlike so many of your
Fellow Americans

I love the way you use aposiopesis
Much more than when you make use of
Antirrhesis

If you want to get with me
You better have a
Rhetorical Figure, a
Rhetorical Figure, if
You want to get up ON
This you better have a
Rhetorical Figure, A
Rhetorical Figure
If you want to know the truth
I PREFER a Rhetorical Figure
A Rhetorical Figure
If you want to get up ON this
You better have a Rhetorical Figure
A Rhetorical Figure

Rhetorical Figure (Rhetorical Figure)
Rhetorical Figure (Rhetorical Figure)

So many people chasin' Sacagaweas
Me I'd rather have a bunch of
Onomatopeias baby.
Thwap Splat Gurgle Gurgle
Thwap Splat Gurgle Gurgle
Thwap Splat Gurgle Gurgle
Thwap Splat Gurgle Gurgle

22.
ZOLO

72
DIVIETO
DI SOSTA
ROMA
MERDA

Just So You Know

Life Is a Battlefield Each Day
Yeah "Who's the New Guy"
You might say
There were times I didn't think
That I would make it
I thought I'd never understand

And even know it's still not over
I still get my DQ on with some frequency
No, I don't mean Dairy Queen
I covered that on album 3

Just So You Know
I always knew that you loved me
Let there be no doubt
Or confusion in your brain

Just So You Know
I always felt it that you loved me
Every single minute, of every single
Solitary day

And you've had a hard road of your own
But you never bellyached or groaned
Sometimes, you didn't know where you
Were goin'
But you never lost your way
And I know at times it hurt to see
How my troubled mind could put
The hurts on me
But you never put me down
You were gentle, strong and kind

The trogs'll probably hear this and think "what a bore"
But they probably never met someone like you before
They probably don't even know how to parallel park
They probably don't even pick up their dog's poop in the park
Or anywhere else, for that matter
And their probably, emotionally constipated
Just like me, when I was 3

Just So You Know
I always knew that you loved me
Let there be no doubt
Or confusion in your brain

Just So You Know
I always felt it that you loved me
Every single minute, of every single
Solitary day

Just So You Know
I always knew that you loved me
Let there be no doubt or confusion
In your mind

I always felt it so deeply that you loved me

Dandy Star

There is an eerie silence in this house tonight
I feel the weight of time, the hours pass so slowly

I hear the sounds of morning, but my eyes can't see
Death arrived last night and lies sleeping next to me

Chorus:
You in all my dreams
I rush to meet you in the morning
I see your breath, rolling, curling
In the cold, crisp air
Oh Dandy Star
It's you, who carries me though
Dew-soaked meadows
Out and away from the horror of this place

Aunty Betty's in the parlor
Sitting in her favorite chair
I feel her eyes wide open
Frozen in a lifeless stare
As fear takes over, I retreat
Into my mind
And there you are, my Dandy Star
Forever, by my side

I always knew you would return to take me
From this place

Your Portfolio

Your portfolio
Is much bigger than I thought
Your portfolio
Is much bigger than I had anticipated
It gets swollen and inflated

Your portfolio
Is making me wet
It makes me want to fall
Even deeper into debt

Your portfolio
Has razor-sharp claws
But that just makes me excited
Instead of giving me pause

Automatic perfection
Information technology
Strict Foreclosure
Authorization Validity Check
Hostile Takeover
Statutory Instrument
Non-performing Asset
I hope this is what you meant

Некогда не извиняйтесь за то,
Чем вы стали
Всё что мы имеем
Заработали потом и кровью

(Never apologize for what
you've become
Everything we have we've
earned
With blood and sweat)

Your portfolio
Has killed and it will kill again
I can't wait to feel it
Rubbing up against my skin

Your portfolio
Is leaking all over the floor
Your portfolio
Is making me feel like I want
more

Your portfolio
Is saying all of THE right
things
But when it doesn't call me
back
My feelings are hurt and it
stings

Your portfolio
Has been seen carousing
Out on the town
Makes me wonder why I
waited UP
All decked out like a clown

The Only Baby

So you ventured out into the new world
To spread your seed in every land you could find
To take by force, whatever you could get your hands
You said: "We're gonna take whatever place, on the
Map my finger lands on"

We'll show them savages, who's calling all the shots
We'll give them education, which they could not have
Got without us
We'll strip the land, and force her to put out
And if we don't get what we want
We'll put it in her mouth

This is really hard
I think we're gonna need some slaves
We'll drag some people back to here
And we'll make them dig their very own
Graves
We'll give them clothes, and teach them
To behave
And they will like it or else, because God
Obviously wants it that way.

This should destroy their spirits and crush
Their sense of self

And when we see the effect this has
We'll blame it on the people themselves.
And if they complain, we'll pour an ocean's
Worth of sugar and drugs on top
And then we'll get some bald guy
Wearing a suit to go on tv and berate them
When they cannot stop

And we'll shun the ones, who do not get the
Christian diseases, like: cancer, ms, heart failure
Lou Gehrig's codependency and diabetes
We know which ones come from our father in the sky
And we know which ones were designed by the other Guy

That THING in the White House
Is beholden to a Deity
It's the same one we are
And it's name is the Economy
Imaginary numbers dance like
Vegas Showgirls in his head
And when the veil is lifted
You're gonna wish that you were dead

And now we've gotten all the things we
Could ever want

WATER

BRITISH EXTRACTING Co
Tel Fax
01482 225198

Like cars, milk frothers, crime and books from
Self-help authors
And coal and diamonds, buildings, oil and
Lots of steel
And every moment was worth it
I'm sorry, that's just how I feel

Well that's the only baby that bitch could have
That's the only baby that bitch could have
Don't look so glum, there's no reason to be sad
'Cause baby that's the only baby
That bitch could've ever had.

Billy

Billy as the world tries hard to
Cheat death once again, I've
Got some extra time which I thought
That I would spend by
Working on your song, and
It's shameful and I'm sorry that it's
Taken me so long

Billy you are always on my mind
And I think back to
When I first laid eyes on you at
Paris On The Platte, I
Saw you walking in
And immediately fell victim
To your, tractor-beam-like grin

Billy, we're so different but
I think you must agree
That we could not support
The weight of expectation
And it forced us to our knees
And we set about destroying ourselves
As members of the cult
members of the cult
members of the cult
Of masculinity

Billy I remember how you let me
Stay at your place
As a birthday gift it was
On the night of July, 25th
And we both slept in the same bed
You didn't care you let me know
That you were not afraid

Billy you have always
Made me feel like royalty
And I, always looked up to you
And you always made me feel
Like I was loved
But then I had to walk away
Because I knew that I would
Follow you, right to my own grave

Billy, we're so different
But I think you must agree
That we're both disappointments
To so many folks in this society
So we continue with the task
Of punishing ourselves
But maybe you don't think I'm weak
And maybe someday soon we'll speak

Just like we used to do,
When you were you
And I was me

Billy, we're so different but
I think you must agree
That we could not support
The weight of expectation
And it forced us to our knees
And we set about destroying ourselves
As members of the cult
members of the cult
members of the cult
Of masculinity

The Art of the Lie

All That School For Nothing

I lost my patience several decades ago
Around the time I was in utero
They taught me all about hyenas and vultures
I saw them worshipping their tyrants with sculptures

It takes Olympic-level instestinal fortitude
To watch what you are doing to your food
I'd rather watch a seagull swallow a rabbit
You see an opportunity so you grab it

All that school for nothin'
Heavens to Betsy, Baby, you're really something
All that therapy and money down the toilet
I could tell you your future, but I don't wanna
Spoil it

I got the seven-year itch about two minutes in
When they told me 'bout the concept of original sin
I learned a lot watching the films of S. Kubrick
I saw them worshipping large pieces of fabric

You're not honest, you're just a pric
The personification (human version) of a selfie stick

Marbles

I've got the poise
Of a newborn giraffe
And I feel like I've
Fallen off the wagon
My moves are quite clearly
Unchoreographed
My comportment like that
of a Komodo dragon

You make me lose my marbles
You get me all worked up into a lather
My words are coming out in
Fits and garbles
There's no one on this Earth
With whom I'd rather

You deactivate
My defense mechanisms
I think I'm coming unglued
I have emotional whiplash
I cannot brandish my trademark
Aloof cynicism
I've taken up macramé
Just to deal with the backlash

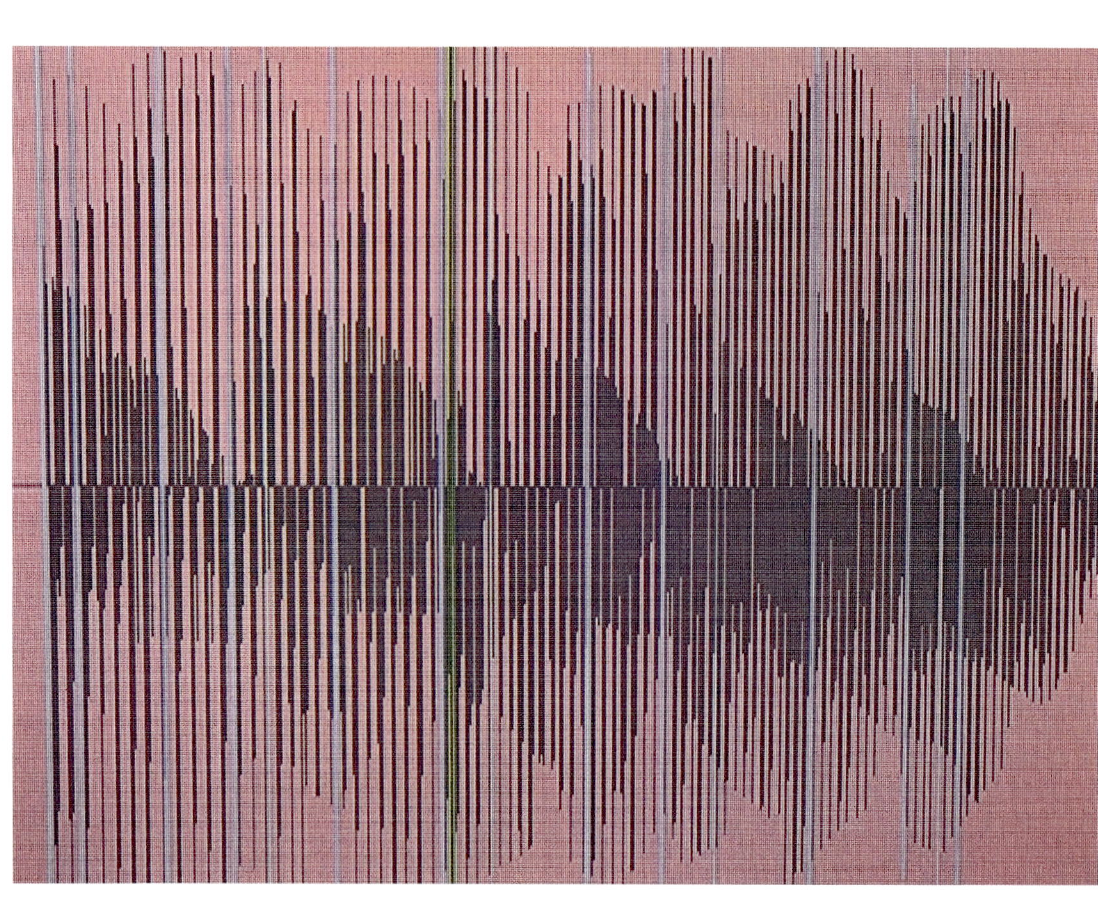

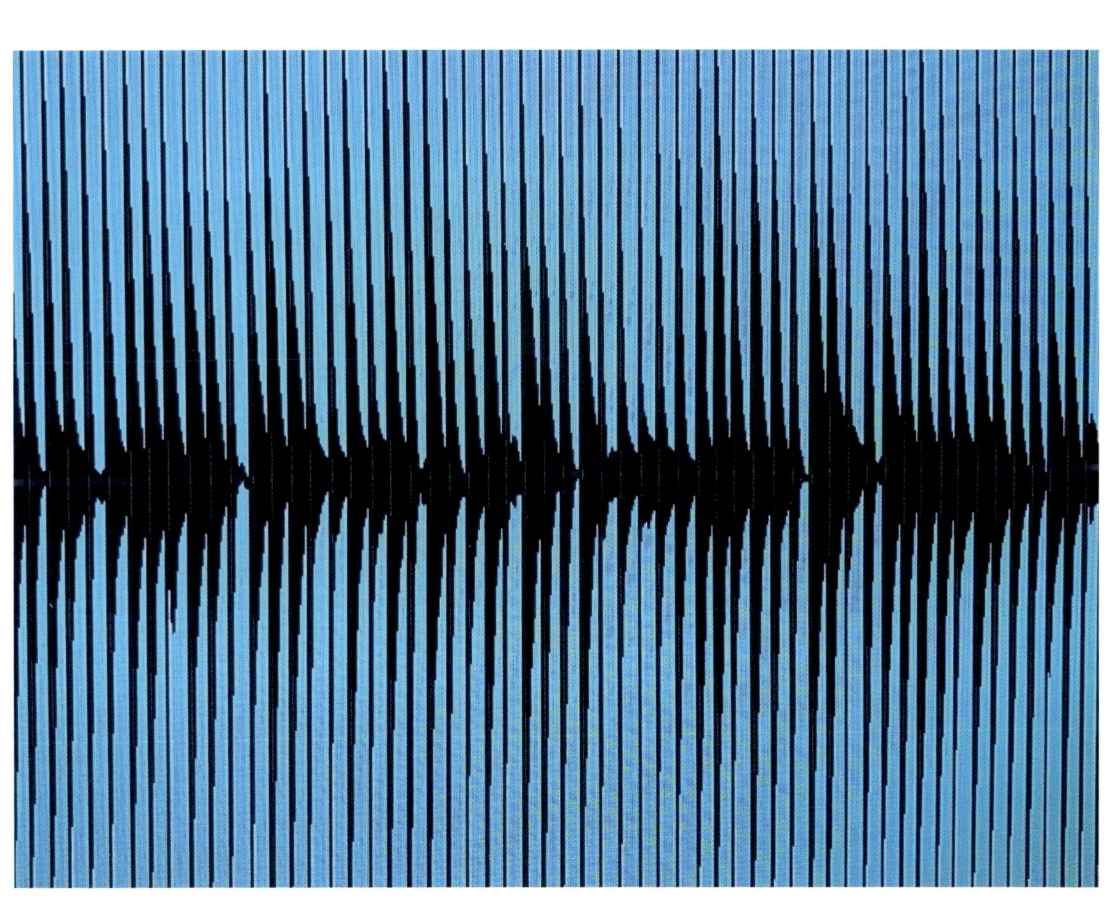

Father

I looked across the street
It's winter, there's a soft snow falling
The doors are open, there's no light
I hear a faint voice calling me
We walk inside into those rooms
Where we once laughed and played
It's all empty now, but it feels like it
Was yesterday

I see that cubbyhole and where
We used to eat together
I see the walls you built
The room where I slept as a child
I went downstairs into the basement
Even though the lights aren't on
I can hear the Beach Boys singin'
And my brothers playin' pool

And sometimes I just want to run into your arms
And let you hold me, once again
I feel ashamed because I couldn't be the man
You always hoped that I, would become
Ahh, Ahh

And there's the staircase where I sat back in the 70s
Listening to the radio, the first big hit from C&T
I'd still be sitting there, if anything were up to me
I can hear you telling me that nothing on this Earth
Is Free

And now I see the workbench that you made
With your two hands
And I'd give anything, to see you standing
Where you used to stand
To feel your hand upon my shoulder
That meant comfort then
To see you turn around and smile and say
"Hey Cuatro, how you been"

So you've dedicated your entire life
To one big lie it seems
You are afraid to live, and equally afraid to die
You imparted that to me, I ate it up
And swore that I
Would never take part in this world
Or try to build a life

And the people who sang "Jesus loves me
This I know"
Have chosen someone else and say
The Bible told them so
The laws of men aren't good enough for them
They want their Book to be
The only one allowed, but, not all of it
Just the OT

Mother and Son

What was it like when you welcomed your son on that day
Mother
Did your love eclipse everything you'd ever known, before him
You know the world is a rough place to be don't you
Mother
You held him close to your heart safe from harm as you prayed
Mother

What was it like when you sent him off into the world
Mother
They say the bond between Mother and Child is an
Indestructible thing
He wants to fight for his country the noblest of things
Mother
He left to sail the vast oceans in search of his dreams
Mother

GATE N°5

THREE BILLBOARDS
LOVING VINCENT
THE ROOM FRI
RHPS SAT
ESQUIRE

He doesn't know hate now
He doesn't know sorrow
He doesn't know fear
Nor does he
Fret for tomorrow
He doesn't feel pain anymore
He doesn't feel any shame
He knows what men spend their lives
In pursuit of
He is at peace while their writhe
In their horror

Did you know it inside of your heart when he died
Mother
They took his life with an inhuman rage because
His love was different from theirs
Now they don't want to face what they've done do they
Mother
His life meant nothing to those who would judge him that day
Mother

Meek AF

I know that you
Think you're really smooth
You think you're
One of the sheep
But you also think
That you're the GOAT
You're sure that's why
You got the job
You killed your audition
For the village mob
You think you understand
But the chances of that
Are really very remote

You don't believe
Anything you read
In the Good Book
That's not a Good Look
For you
Your spirit animal's a bulldozer
You're Shelly the Machine
But you wanna be a closer
'Cause Jesus wants you rich
The art of the lie, the old
Bait and switch

You are so super meek
You think people like me
Are weak
You are so super meek
Your super hotrod's super
sleek
You're gonna mow them
losers down
No weak folks here while
you're around
You're grinnin' because you're
winnin'

Your wife knows you're not
kidding
So she always does your
bidding
Because she thinks
You really love her
No son of yours will ever be a
fag
Even if you have to drag him
Around the town behind your
truck

Your favorite party game is
Twistin' Scriptures!
You never read the NT 'cause
there weren't
Enough pictures
God's just a bit too slow for
you
You're gonna build your
kingdom here
If it's the last thing you DO
You're sprit animal's a giant
bulldozer
You're Shelly the Machine
But you wanna be a closer
'Cause everybody knows that
Jesus
Wants you rich
It's the Art of the Lie
Your new sales pitch

It's a Bitch

I was examining the walls of my encephalon
Dreaming of hot heshers playing Robotron
I was
Luxuriating on the davenport
Flagillating myself like it was
Some kind of sport
Well that's a bitch
Yeah baby that's a bitch
Come on sugar that's a bitch
Come on baby that's a bitch

I was deep within the bowels of the establishment
Wondering how I'm ever gonna pay the rent
I was
Boning UP on my Icelandic declensions
When the landlord rang me up and said you
Don't get no extentions that's a bitch
Come on baby, that's a bitch
Come on suga that's a bitch
Come on baby that's a bitch

I am feeling an unmistakable cacoethes
For some fellowship with some sort of less
Perceptive species
I am feeling an itch in my medulla oblongata

BITE
ME

Yeah, it happens a lot
The doctor says I gotta lotta 'magination
That could lead to extended bouts of frustration
I'm losing patience
It's a classic demonstration
That it's a bitch

Bom bom, bom bom, etc.

I was rehearsing my phillipic
It's going to be terrific
They will get a dressing down
That'll be apocalyptic
I was wondrin' if I should begin
To decathect
'Cause I am feeling too attached
I want to disconnect
I was availing myself
Of some old school neuroses
When a fella on the radio
Said "Bella Lugosi's Dead"
Ooooooooo, baby that's a bitch

That's a bitch, that's a bitch
That's a stone-cold bitch
That's a bitch, that's a bitch
That's a stone-cold bitch
That's a bitch, that's a bitch
That's a stone-cold bitch
That's a bitch, that's a bitch
That's a stone-cold bitch

Huh, huh, huh
Hah, hah, hah

Daddy

You are calm
You are rage
You were there
Yesterday
You will be
There tomorrow
Nothing more
Left to say

Unattainable
You're Unobtanium
What have you done
To my cranium
I'm so tired
Will you hold me
I just want
You to mold me

Daddy, you're like the ocean
You're like the waves crashing
On the beach that morning
Daddy, you are majestic
Would you betray me?
Would you hurt me?

You don't like
What I am
I have come
To understand
It's not like
They all think
Like in Monster
At the skating rink
I can rest
When I'm with you
Be myself
Let you do
What you do
Perfect form
Perfect love
Perfect safety
From above

It's no fault
Of yours or mine
There would always
Come a time
You'd deliver
Me to them
For what I am
Is a sin

The Child Catcher

Remember when
You'd never heard of him
Your first reaction might have been
To smile
Once upon a time
Your unadulterated mind
Could not conceive of something
Of this kind
That you would wither and die
On the vine
Alabaster demon
Transmogrifying semen
Now was this in the agreement
Now I understand what she meant
Blood-soaked pathogen
Tied for first place with original sin
I really wish I'd never let him in
Now I can feel him deep beneath
My skin

The Child Catcher is alive
His shape is shifting right
Before your eyes again
He's always been there
In the shadows calling out

Your name
When he gets hold of you
No thing will ever be the same
The Child Catcher has arrived
And now he doesn't ever
Have to hide again
He beckons you to come inside
His brightly colored carriage
That's where the coupling happens
Ending in a deadly marriage

The perfect time
To take control of minds
A recent scientific study finds
Is in the womb
Life nipped in the bud
Delivered subtly through
The mother's own blood
You'll never know exactly
What it was
The happy nest becomes
The perfect tomb

Leon's
FROZEN
CUSTARD
SHAKES
MALTS
CONES
PINTS
QUARTS
SODAS
SUNDAES
LEON'S
SUPER SUNDAE
Special
$5.30

Court
Pastry
Italian
Ices

Laura Lou

Laura Lou lemon bar
I don't know
Where you are
Enter now
I submit
Autumn's coming
We both know it
Ahhhh

Laura Lou
Southern belle
They keep saying
We're going to hell
Jessica is Joseph S.
Life was never
Not a mess
Ahhhh

Laura Lou, Buffalo
Can't remember
Do you like snow
Springtime in
The Southland is best
Indigo, Cintra test
Ahhhh

Zeitgeist

The world is closing in again on me tonight
And I can see it's gonna be a long way to the morning light
And I'm not tryin' to lay some heavy trip on you
As some folks say I tend to do
When I forget myself as I do do

The world keeps telling me that
I don't need to be with anybody
I am all I need unto myself
I think they have been misinformed
Their formulas won't weather storms
This zeitgeist fruit is full of worms
And in the end I know that I need you

The way you move around in this world
Makes it so that I
Can navigate the darkened recesses
Of my beleaguered mind
I've had to up my game
Emotionally speaking
Though I be hard pressed to say
That that has not come in quite handy

For it makes it possible for me
To understand in a way that I had
Not done heretofor
Barbara says I'm going to fast
I'm just afraid that this won't last
I feel that it is my main task
To make sure that you know that I love you

The world is closing in again on me tonight
And I can see it's gonna be a long way
To the morning light